Love Won Another

Love Won Another

Every Christian's Guide to Evangelism

Lewis and Molly Misselbrook

Marshall Pickering

Marshall Morgan and Scott
Marshall Pickering
3 Beggarwood Lane, Basingstoke, Hants RG23 7LP, UK

Copyright © 1987 by Lewis and Molly Misselbrook
First published in 1987 by Marshall Morgan and Scott
Publications Ltd
Part of the Marshall Pickering Holdings Group
A subsidiary of the Zondervan Corporation

British Library Cataloguing in Publication Data

Misselbrook, Lewis
  Love won another.
  I. Tile II. Misselbrook, Molly
  248'.5   BV4520

  ISBN 0–551–01429–6

Text phototypeset in Plantin 10 on 11 pt
by Input Typesetting Ltd, London SW19 8DR
Printed in Great Britain by
Anchor Brendon Ltd, Tiptree, Essex

Dedicated to
Our three boys and their families:

Christopher, the Craftsman and Designer

Peter, the Pastor, with Liz, Abigail and Jenny

David, the Doctor, with Ruth, Clare and Tom

All a warmth and joy to our hearts.

Contents

Introduction

This is a book full of stories of people and churches. This is where our life and ministry have been.

We were both born at Ware in Hertfordshire, were both in the Air Force during the Second World War but did not meet until just after the war – and that was in a team for Christian witness. The first church we served was the Leavesden Road Baptist Church in Watford, a church full of loving, praying people, and we owe them a great deal of love and gratitude. Our second church was in Rushden, Northants, and there, in a lovely old manse of thirteen rooms, our children grew up.

Our third adventure was to plant a church in the new estate at Chelmsley Wood, near Birmingham. The estate grew from nothing to sixty thousand people in five years and we lived and grew with them. Then began nine years' service when as Field Worker and Adviser in Evangelism for the Baptist Union of Great Britain and Ireland we travelled the whole of England and part of Wales.

Finally we came as Consultants in Mission to the Baptist Union of Scotland and we were fully involved as Field Workers in the great movement of Scotreach, a three-year plan of outreach. Whilst doing this we have travelled through Scotland and its islands.

We have had an active and exciting life and we hope some of the love and excitement and gratitude for the grace and goodness of God shows through these pages.

The Love Won Another course was a training course for Scotreach and we taught it in thirteen centres throughout Scotland. But we have also taught much of what is included in it in England and Wales in numerous churches and conferences and in our lectures to students at Spurgeon's College and at Cardiff and Regent's Park Colleges. We remember with great warmth of heart all those churches and all of God's Beautiful People with whom we have had fellowship.

Our method of writing this book has been that one of us would write the draft of a chapter, the other would read and criticise it and then it would be rewritten. Molly initially wrote chapters 5 and 8 (which she led and taught in the course) and Lewis wrote the drafts for the other chapters. For the most part we have written as a pair (the 'we' passages) but from time to time a personal piece comes through. As far as the Group Exercises at the end of each chapter are concerned we do assume that everyone in the group has their own personal copy of this book.

There is no copyright on the appendices but we would ask for a printed acknowledgement whenever they are reproduced.

We are deeply grateful to:

Christine Whitell, editor of Marshall Pickering Books. Without her encouragement this book would not have been written.

Peter Barber, General Secretary of the Baptist Union of Scotland, and Tom Rogers, Secretary for Evangelism for the Baptist Union of Great Britain and Ireland, who have read the script and made valuable comments.

Richard Bewes, Rector of All Souls Church, Langham Place, and Clive Calver, General Secretary of the Evangelical Alliance, who have seen the script and given it a commendation.

Morag Gunn, who found time in a busy life to type it up for us with her usual cheerfulness and efficiency.

We hope the sharing of our thought and experience will be of inspiration and help to others and will encourage them to love and pray, to live greatly and to witness naturally in the Spirit of Jesus.

Lewis and Molly Misselbrook
July 1986

Part I:

Medium and Message

Chapter 1: Preparing the Church for Witness

The witness that changes people's lives is something you cannot contrive, manufacture or command. It comes from a Spirit you receive as a gift, a Spirit that changes your life first.

It is the overflowing of the heart of God into a human heart or into a community of God's people and filling it so full of Jesus and His love that it cannot possibly be kept in but overflows again and ever must, for that is its nature.

For that reason it is not possible to give a list of procedures and techniques that will guarantee 'success'. Nevertheless there are churches all over the country that have sprung into new life and witness in the last twenty years. The reason for this cannot be simply explained geographically or socially for there is no situation, be it in an inner city, new estate, rural or anywhere else, where we have not some churches showing life and growth. But from them all some characteristics seem to stand out. These are what we intend now to look at.

Expect great things from God

We British people are by nature negative thinkers. Travelling throughout Britain, helping groups of church people in their witness to Jesus, we often give them a test. (You can try it yourself.) We say to them, 'Close your eyes for a moment. Think of something in your life or character – any trait, characteristic, attitude or value – that occupies your mind more than anything else.' We give them a moment and then say, 'Right. Open your eyes. Hands up everyone who has thought of something good, great or wonderful that you praise the Lord for'. We usually get about four hands up in every one hundred people!

We are, as churches, problem-centred and not Jesus-centred. If only we could fix our eyes upon Jesus, upon His purpose, His power, His glory and grace many of our problems would disappear and the others we would tackle with a new spirit. In the past Christians have suffered from a failure syndrome and some find it hard to escape from it. We often ask church people 'Where do you think your church will be three years from now?' Only too often the reply is in negative terms – 'I hope we will not have lost too many members' or 'I hope we will be able to hold on to those we have'. Just keeping the wheels turning has taken over from the spirit of mission.

In our work of training in evangelism we include door-to-door visitation. We give a group some training and then lead them out to practise what we have taught. We both take one other person with us. We go to three or four doors and talk to folk while our trainee watches and listens. Then we will say to him or her, 'Would you like to lead in the next one and I will stand by to come in if you want me to'.

They swallow hard and say, 'Oh, alright. Yes'.

They knock on the next door and then happens what we call 'the doorstep droop'. The whole body sags! When the door opens they say everything correctly – in fact sometimes like a parrot – but are unaware that their face and body are also speaking, and speaking powerfully. Their lips are speaking of love and care and of Jesus. Their bodies are saying 'I'm terribly sorry. I've come to talk to you about religion and I know you are not going to be interested and I'm very embarrassed about it myself'. And they are then surprised that the reply is negative or one of withdrawal or suspicion!

In fact they have projected a *No* on the whole situation. If they had really believed that the greatest miracle in the world is the miracle of God's love and mercy in the midst of a world like this and the most wonderful thing they could offer another person was the grace of God in Jesus Christ, then their faces and bodies would say that. They would project a great and glad *Yes* upon the situation.

A few years ago *The Readers Digest* printed an article by Robert Rosenthall, an educational psychiatrist. He taught educational psychiatry to a group and at one time gave them each a rat which they were to train to get through a particular maze. To half the class he said, 'Your rats, for genetic reasons, will be very poor at finding their way through a maze'. To the other half he said, 'Your rats, for genetic reasons, will be particularly good at finding their way through a maze'. When the students had had time to train their rats, they were all tested and the rats Robert Rosenthall had said would be good were very much better than those he said would be poor. He then revealed that he knew nothing about the rats and their genes.

The difference was not in the rats but in the expectations of the trainers. Those who expected their rats to be poor had spent little time or energy training them – what was the point? They were going to be poor anyway. But those who expected their rats to be good spent endless time and trouble training them that they might excel. Rosenthall ended the article with the pointed question, 'How many children are there in our schools who do not do very well because no-one expects them to?'

When I read that article I said, 'And how many churches are there whom God is not able to bless very much because they do not expect any blessing?'

Our first need is to expect great things from God.

Get God's view of witness

Any page of the New Testament will show that the early Christians felt it was their responsibility to share the gospel with those who were not Christians. When you look at the churches today it would appear that too often Christians feel it is the responsibility of non-Christians to bring themselves into a church building to hear the gospel from the preacher. We have inverted the whole movement of witness. The New Testament Church, however, was one dynamic *outgoing* missionary movement. Its members believed that in the death and resurrection of Jesus man's salvation was effected and forgiveness and new life in Christ were offered free to all. He had transformed their own existence and now the animating power of His love drove them out into all the world to share the Good News with every creature. They had a message both to live and to deliver, a commission to fulfil and the power of His Spirit was upon them for its fulfilment.

Jerome, in the fourth century, described baptism as the ordination of the laity and it is evident that in early times the amazing spread of Christianity was very largely due to the lives and witness of ordinary Christian people. Wherever they were they 'gossipped Christ' in the most natural and contagious way.

Jim Peterson, in his book *Evangelism as a Lifestyle*[1] tells of a time when he was travelling by ship to Brazil. On board were sixty tourists and sixty missionaries. Jim Peterson mixed with the tourists and often found himself naturally and happily sharing his faith. He felt that with sixty missionaries and sixty tourists surely none of the tourists could leave the ship without a great exposure to the Christian message. Instead he found most missionaries staying together in their own groups and when he shared his excitement about witness they arranged a meeting on board so that the gospel could be preached to the tourists!

Our commission as Christians – every one of us – is to live the Jesus-life daily out there in the world in a natural, friendly and committed lifestyle and to speak genuinely, lovingly and honestly of Him whenever it is appropriate and opportune. It is useless to dream of being a missionary in Brazil if those we meet every day are not seeing the beauty of Jesus in our lives and not hearing His invitation through our lips.

Perhaps a great deal of our fear of sharing our faith would be dispelled if we could understand witnessing as just being Christian and being honest and open to Jesus and to others in the ordinary run of everyday life. We become fearful and often come to grief in our witness when we see it as something we have to try to do over and above our daily living and sharing. We recently met a lady who told us of how new freedom and blessing had come to her life when she gave up 'trying to witness'. 'It nearly ruined my life and all my relationships', she said. 'I was not able to enjoy people and really listen to them because I was always worrying about how I could get my "witness" in'.

She was then told to stop trying to make opportunities and simply to take the opportunities God gave her. Each morning she asked the Lord for His appointments for her. 'The very first day,' she said, 'I was in a Post Office and got chatting to an old lady waiting to draw her pension. She confided that she came from a poor area but always travelled to this Post Office in a high class area because it made her feel Somebody. Before I thought about it I said, "I'm a princess". She said, "You're not, are you?" I then told her I was a daughter of the King – of the King of Kings – and had a wonderful time telling her about Jesus because she wanted to know. 'Then only two days later I was in a shop. The girl serving me kept looking over her shoulder. "I'm sorry," she said, "but I keep feeling that someone is calling my name". "Oh," I said to her, "that's just like Samuel". She looked puzzled and asked me who Samuel was. I told her Samuel was in the Bible and how God had called to him. She was most interested and came from behind the counter to talk with me. We talked for twenty minutes before another customer came in. I just made an appointment to meet her again. She really did want to know about God. If this is witness I wish someone had told me about it before. It is so natural and so wonderful and I don't have to try any more.'

Sometimes, however, we destroy true witness by attempting to do God's part for Him and neglecting the part He has told us to do.

Have clear aims

We sometimes help churches to carry out a survey both of the church and its neighbourhood. We begin by spending two hours with the minister discovering how he sees the church, what its neighbourhood context is and how he sees the church within its neighbourhood. One question we always ask is 'What are your aims?' We ask the same question of the church leaders, organisation leaders and some of the church members. When we look at the results we often find that the minister has one set of aims, the church leaders have another set, the members a third set and every organisation leader his own aims unrelated to any of the others!

Now as Plato pointed out many years ago, if you have a chariot pulled by six horses all pulling in different directions, that chariot is not going to go very far. But if you can get all six horses pulling in the same direction that chariot will go far and fast. That is the point of having clear aims which are worked out by all, known and accepted by all and to which all work in harmony together.

One church took about a year to work out its aims. At every church meeting and in its house groups time was given to answering the question 'Why did God put our church here in this particular neighbourhood at this particular time?' Towards the end of the year they had large lists of all sorts of ideas and suggestions but finally they whittled them down to three simple statements of purpose:

(a) total commitment to Jesus Christ

(b) total commitment to one another as the People of Jesus

(c) total commitment to work and witness for Jesus.

From that time onward you could ask any church leader or any member from the oldest to the youngest what the aims of their church were and they would rap out these three things. They knew and accepted them because they had been deeply involved in working them out.

They then reorganised church life around three 'commissions' (they were far too wise to call them committees), each concerned to foster and further one of the aims. And everyone in the church was related to one of the commissions according to their gifts.

The commissions worked out objectives (practical and measurable steps) to achieve the aims, and the objectives were revised each year. The church began to grow steadily and then rapidly. All the horses were pulling together! Time spent together on working out the aims of Jesus for our church here and now is time well spent.

Use all the gifts God gives

Paul, in Romans 12, 1 Corinthians 12 and in Ephesians, particularly chapter 4, likens the Church to a body (the body of Christ). The body has many members with many different gifts and functions but it remains one body. The Church is the body in which Jesus lives and through which He is to manifest Himself and do His work.

So 'God Himself has put the body together in such a way. . . . so there is no division in the body' (1 Cor. 12: 24–25). Paul says that the Holy Spirit 'as He wishes' gives a different gift to every church member (verses 7 and 11). Every member has a gift and therefore a part to play in the whole body.

I don't know if you regard Paul as a humorist. On the whole he wasn't. He wasn't married for one thing and that increases your sense of humour no end! But in 1 Corinthians chapter 12, Paul has three lovely little cartoons that are as humorous as they are pointed. The first is of a human foot sitting over in the corner of the room all on its own. Paul says, 'Hello, foot, what are you doing?'

'I'm sulking.'

'Yes, I can see that but what are you sulking for?'

'I'm sulking because I'm not a hand. I don't want to be a foot. I want to be a hand'.

'But my dear foot, if God had wanted you to be a hand, He would have made you a hand, wouldn't He? He wants you to be a foot. He loves you to be a foot. Come on, the body needs a foot as well as a hand and we need you'. So, says Paul, never waste time wishing you were someone else or had some other gift. God has given you your gift and a part to play in His body.

The second cartoon is of a large eye coming down the road all on its own. 'Hello, hello', says Paul. (He should really have said 'Aye, aye'!) 'Who are you?'

'I', says the eye, 'am the whole body.'

'Oh, no, you're not,' says Paul. 'You are a big eye and you might be able to see for fifty miles at your size, but you can't do anything else. You can't touch or taste or smell or handle or hear'. (Don't ask what Paul is doing talking to it if it can't hear!)

So, says Paul, no member can do the work of the whole body – not even if you call him a 'minister'! Nor can a small group do the work of the whole body. Every member is needed.

The third cartoon is when the head says to the foot, 'We don't need you. Buzz off.' (That is not the Author-ised Version but that is what is said.) Just suppose I was standing up and suddenly my feet did go off on their own. I would fall with a terrible flop, for we do need the feet.

So says Paul, you might look round your congregation on a Sunday morning and think to yourself, 'Oh. There is old so-and-so over there. We wouldn't miss him if he never came'. Even more sadly old so-and-so might think to himself, 'They wouldn't miss me if I never came'. But, says Paul, for every one whose gift is not discovered, developed and used within the fellowship, the whole body is impoverished and weakened by that much.

Charles Colson tells of an old lady whose life has been transformed and transforming by writing to people in prison. An old man known to me found new inspiration by becoming a prayer partner in a group supporting two who did door-to-door visitation. There is a part everyone can play. Jesus wants His body to be alive, fit and working in every member.

Hit the positive note

There are leaders who never really become one with their people. They speak to their people as 'you' not 'we'. They constantly chide them and show their disappointment in them and in other circles will criticise them. Such leaders breed depression, guilt and latent hostility in the congregation.

Churches that live and grow have people in leadership who have received the love of God for that particular group of people and understand that the heart of the church's fellowship is the sharing of a common life, the source of which is in God, not in human goodness or effort. Such leadership breeds joy, confidence and hope and fills the church with praise, devotion and love and knows the glory of the presence of Jesus in His Church.

Dr Tony Bashford used to tell a lovely story about his young son. The little lad had just learned to say the

Lord's Prayer (although it did tend to begin 'Our Farver and Auntie Heaven') and loved to join in its recitation in church. One Sunday they were away on holiday and went to a church with which they were not familiar. The small boy waited patiently for the prayer to come and at last it did but in a shortened version, ending at 'deliver us from evil'. When the rest of the congregation stopped at this point the small boy's voice continued on. Then, suddenly aware of his solo, the lad turned to his father and in a shrill voice asked 'Why don't they have any power and glory here, Dad?'

That, as Tony Bashford points out, is a very pertinent question for the church scene today.

Exercises for Groups

1. Things that indicate that there is a harvest to be reaped in a district are:
(a) Churches in the district are growing
(b) Cults are growing
(c) When people are showing an interest – new faces are seen at church
(d) New converts appear amongst local people
(e) People seem dissatisfied
Are any of these signs discernable in your church and locality? What do they mean? What can you do about it?

2. Here are some reasons why the church is not effective in witness. Pick the top three for your church and number them in order.
(a) It does not really relate to people outside
(b) It does not train its members to live and articulate the faith
(c) The leaders do everything
(d) It is too busy with organisations and routine to reach out to others as Jesus commanded

(e) It is afraid of what others will think or say

(f) It has not prepared itself to do what Jesus told us to do.

(g) It is lukewarm and not filled with the Spirit of Jesus

(h) Other reason – write in:

Share, one at a time, your top choice. What can you do to improve things?

3. Work out together a short statement on what you feel should be the aims of your church. Then work out several immediate and practical steps to begin to move towards those aims.

Chapter 2: More Preparation

Provide simple training

If we discovered the gifts of all our members we should find (so we are told by the little research done) that something like six to ten per cent of our members have a gift for evangelism. They ought to be discovered, set free from everything else, trained well and become a group responsible for all the organised evangelism the church does.

But that does not mean that the other ninety per cent have no responsibility for making Jesus known. They are not called to be evangelists but they, and all God's people, are called to be witnesses. All should be ready and prepared to speak a simple and honest word for Jesus in and through everyday life and living. This is not likely to happen unless they are given some training. Some of the chapters of this book, including the exercises, will be useful for that.

Look again at our structures

Most churches are working within an organisational framework which was designed for the last century or the early years of this. Consequently our patterns are never quite relevant and Christians are not growing to apply their faith to daily life and to share it with others.

Many of our churches are structured for mediocrity and not for mission. We aim only to keep things going and are so busy maintaining the pattern that we forget its purpose. As one of our colleagues has said, 'We have a subconscious urge to keep busy so that we do not have time to face up to the things Jesus told us to do'.

Let us here speak of just two things:

1. Our witness is child-centred and therefore unbalanced.
Let us make it clear that we are not denigrating children's work. It is important (although we would wish that Sunday school was still for children of non-Christian parents only and that Christian parents were given training and resources to bring up their own children to see and serve the Lord). But too often children's work is almost the only witness the church has. In that case:
(a) it confirms what most people think about the church – 'It is something for the kids'.
(b) It does damage even to the children's work in that it gives them something to grow out of instead of something to grow into.
(c) It does not reap where God indicates a harvest – which today is among young married couples with children. There is a small but perceptible drift of whole families of this kind into our churches.
(d) It ignores the fact that God placed children into families and did not make them in isolation. If we have five children in a class then we are called to befriend and minister to five families.

2. Organisations sometimes eat people.
What happens, for instance, when one of our organisations loses a leader or some workers? Do we ask God whether He means that organisation to continue? He may not, but many of our people would regard it as heresy to say so! We look frantically around and find some young man who has recently joined the church and has not yet been swallowed up by the organisational rat-race. We press him to come and fill the vacancy – 'We

are in such great need. If you don't do it there is no one else to do the work'.

No one says, 'Stop! Let us first discover what the gifts of this new member are. If they are for this particular work then let him do it. But if they are not, then let the organisation kick and scream as much as it likes but he will do what God has called and gifted him to do and not what the machinery dictates'.

In one church, muscle-bound like so many with a great variety of organisations, we did a careful survey and discovered that in the previous five years, out of the hundreds of men, women and children that passed through their hands, only just over one per cent were converted and became church members.

Organisation is necessary for the Spirit to express Himself relevantly in this world. But organisation needs to be carefully watched because it will always tend to take over and to exist simply to perpetuate itself. Organisation should exist for Christ and the gospel and be ruthlessly pruned or cut out when it ceases to be wide open to the Spirit. It is often the 'good' which prevents God's best.

In our first church and neighbourhood survey we interviewed the lady in charge of the Women's Meeting. We chatted with her and all went well until we asked what was her aim in running this meeting. After a moment's pause she said, 'To keep the meeting going'.

'What for?' we asked.

'Well, to keep the meeting going.'

'But what do you hope will happen in the lives of the forty ladies because of their coming to the meeting each week?'

'Well, it's been going for sixty years so it must be needed.' The idea of any clear aims or purpose had long since ceased to guide this meeting.

A day later we talked to the leader of the men's meeting in the same church. 'What is the aim of your meeting?' we asked and he replied 'To win men for Christ'.

'Wonderful. And how many have you won over the last year?'

'Ah, we haven't won any over the last year'.

'And how many men have you won to Christ over the last five years?'

'Five years. Ah, five years. I don't think we have actually won any during the last five years.'

We had then to suggest that if the men's meeting leaders were serious about wanting to win men for Christ they might look for some more simple or direct way of winning them. In fact, although 'winning men for Christ' was proudly printed as their aim upon their notepaper it had long since ceased to be the aim of the meeting.

We suggest that the leaders of every church organisation, without any pressure or interference from the minister, elders or deacons, should meet once a year (possibly at Church Anniversary time) to face up to and talk through eight questions.

(a) What is our aim?

(b) Is this a New Testament aim?

(c) Are we achieving that aim?

(d) Would there be some more simple and direct method of achieving that aim?

(e) Is our aim and our work a truly integral part of the aim and work of the church?

(f) Are we, as leaders, giving the time and getting the training and refresher courses to be excellent leaders?

(g) If our organisation deals with children, are we including time, prayer and care to work with the families and not just the children in isolation?

(h) Is our organisation tending in any way to exist for itself and its own perpetuation or does it exist solely for Christ and the gospel? Can we lay ourselves and all of it completely at His feet and utterly at His disposal?

Prayer

No great thing is ever done for God without prayer. For the truth is that in the spiritual sphere God is always the initiator and the doer and we are but the channels of His purpose and power.

Again and again we have been to churches which are experiencing new life and blessing and have sought to find how it all began. Almost always it has been traced back to the church driven to prayer or to a small praying group. I speak with feeling about prayer because I am a child of prayer. I was born into a divided home. My mother was a beautiful Christian and my father was a hard agnostic. When I was four my mother managed to get me smuggled off to Sunday school and my father turned a blind eye to it as long as I never mentioned it.

When I was thirteen I left Sunday school – everybody did. I reckoned that I had had my ration of God and had been innoculated against it for the rest of my life. But when I was seventeen our family moved to another town and my mother found a church there that was a real blessing to her.

One Sunday evening she said to me, 'Lewis, will you come with me?' and I replied 'Not on your life'. The tears began to run down my mother's cheeks and in the end, because I loved my mum, I said 'Oh alright, I'll come'. And I went.

That night I felt God saying in my heart, 'I want you. I want your life'. I stuck it out for another two Sunday evenings and each time the same thing happened. Then I simply knelt at my bedside and said, 'Lord, I don't know why you want me. But for what this life of mine is worth, I give it to you. Please cleanse it, fill it with your Spirit and use it for your purpose'. In so unremarkable a fashion was the beginning of my Christian life.

Just after I was converted the Second World War broke out. I joined the Air Force and went to Canada for training. There I met some wonderful Christian people, including one young man in the Canadian Air Force, who in the course of time came to this country and visited my home. I was not there but my parents were, and my mother, in good British fashion went to make him a cup of tea. He was left with my dad and, assuming my father was a Christian, began to share with him some of the things Jesus had done in his life. Had it been anyone else my father would have said, 'You had better shut up or you'll be in for trouble'. As it was he simply stood and listened, not saying a word.

A few weeks later, on a Sunday evening, he said to my mum, 'I think I'll come to church with you this evening'. If there was anything guaranteed to make my mum die on the spot that was it! But she survived and the two of them went to church and soon after Jesus Christ changed my dad's life and filled it with His love.

Behind that miracle was my mother, living the Jesus-life in our home day after day and always bringing us to God in her prayers. There must have been a thousand times when the devil said to her, 'What's the use of praying? You have been praying for that man for nearly thirty years and he is as hard as ever. As for your son, he is going the same way. Give it up'. But she carried on praying and living out the love of Jesus and where there is love and prayer God's miracles happen. Our part is to love, pray and witness. It is His part to change lives. We cannot do that but when we pray we open the door to let Jesus in.

There are some people you cannot speak to for Jesus. You would put them further off if you tried. But nothing can stop you loving them and nothing can stop you praying for them.

The will to venture

Most Christians enjoy books and courses on Christian witness – so long as they do not have to venture out to do something about it!

One of the Argos posters[2] shows a ship on the high seas and underneath are the words 'A ship in a harbour is safe, but that's not what ships are for'.

Our business as Christians is not to stay safe in the harbour of the church fellowship but to venture out onto the high seas of daily life, there living out the Jesus-life, loving, praying, serving, asking God for His opportunities to speak a word for Jesus and ready to do so lovingly, humbly and joyfully when the opportunity is given.

It is usually the most 'ordinary' people that God uses greatly. Our first church was a tremendous blessing to us. It was full of loving, praying people. In our first year there God said to us all, 'I have not given you all this love and blessing just to keep to yourselves. Let it flow out to the whole neighbourhood'.

So the deacons thought and prayed together to find what God would have us do right there. Finally we sent out a warm, caring letter once a month for six months to four thousand homes in the neighbourhood. We also sent a monthly letter to every church member to keep them in touch with the vision and plans. Then we sent out our members two-by-two to knock on every door and make a loving contact with people in a "Mission of Friendship".

We asked for volunteers for the visiting and 110 responded. They were given simple training and on the last evening we asked them to pair themselves off and we would give each pair three addresses to visit in the first month. (If they made a good contact they could have that again as one of their three visits for the next month but three visits a month was all each pair would have until the whole area was visited. That took over three years.)

As the pairs came for their addresses I noticed one pair who made my heart fall into my boots. One was a middle-aged man but immature as a Christian and with a gift (or ungift) for not explaining things well. When he explained something to you, you were usually a lot more clear when he began than when he finished! And he had paired himself off with another middle-aged man who had a long, dismal face rather like that of a blood-hound. Not exactly the kind of face you would send to commend anything, much less Christianity.

As they came forward the thought went through my mind to say to them 'Brothers, you just pray for us and the rest of us will do the visiting'. But after all this build-up I hadn't the nerve and weakly gave them three addresses but thinking 'Lord, preserve us, or them, or the people they visit – whichever may need it most'.

Off they went and appeared at our door the next evening to report. As soon as I saw them I thought, 'Oh dear. They would be the first pair back'. Then I noticed their glowing faces and heard their story.

They had gone off to the first address earlier that evening and as they went they remembered the instruction in the training class 'As you go, pray'. They discussed this for some time and in the end discovered that the only thing they both really wanted to pray for was that the people might be out!

They got to the door and one knocked and then they both leant against each other for support. The door opened and there stood a lady with dirty hands. 'Please,' they began, 'We are from the church in Leavesden Road and we are on our Mission of Friendship'.

'I'm sorry,' said the lady, 'but I've no time to bother with you now. I've only just got home and my stove has broken down and I'm just trying to mend it'.

That was her famous mistake because the man with the sad face worked in a shop that sold stoves. 'I'll mend it,' he said, and in he went before she had a chance to consider his offer. The stove needed only a minor adjustment which he did on the spot! She got the stove going, made them a cup of tea and there were the three of them sitting round the kitchen table drinking tea and chatting happily.

A pause came in the conversation as she asked, 'Oh, yes, what was it you came for?' And suddenly they remembered – Mission!

As well as they could this pair told the lady what Jesus meant to them. Later she said she had never felt so moved in all her life. Never had she dreamt that two such unlikely men would come and sit at her kitchen table and talk about Jesus Christ in such an honest and personal way.

Not only did this lady become a Christian (although not on this first visit) but this pair – the pair I would never have chosen – became our star pair in the visiting. They were asked into thirty per cent of the homes they visited and God blessed and used them past all our (and their) imagining. God did not use the glib speakers. He used those who could not speak easily but in whose hearts there was some deep and rich vein of love and genuine blessing of Jesus that communicated itself past all their speaking.

If you feel that you are not the kind of person God can use greatly in Christian witness, you may be the very one He can use most.

Group exercises

1. In what ways do we think the presence of our church is making faith a live option or a real possibility for others? How could we improve?

2. Are we substituting the church gathered for worship as the primary place to preach the gospel, instead of a place to develop mature Christians who will be a demonstration of the presence of Jesus to the world and a

source of live Christian witness through every member every day? Can we improve?

3. Are we reaching out to families with the gospel, parents first, or taking the easy but unsatisfactory path of seeking only to win children? Is there action we should take?

4. Are we discovering, developing and deploying those who have a gift for evangelism, setting them free from everything else to work as a group? Should we do something about this?

Chapter 3: What Is the Gospel?

The word 'gospel' simply means 'good speil' or 'good news'. But what is the good news?

Definitions of the gospel

Dr C H Dodd, a great New Testament scholar, attempted to discover the good news the first Apostles preached by examining the preaching reported in the Acts and the Epistles in his book *The Apostolic Preaching and Its Developments*[3]. His findings may be summed up in eight points:

(a) Jesus is the Christ, the Messiah, the promised One of God.

(b) He lived a life of love among us and 'went about doing good'.

(c) He died for our sins.

(d) He rose again. Death could not hold him.

(e) He is ascended to God's right hand, the place of authority.

(f) He sends the Holy Spirit – His own Spirit – upon those who put their trust in Him.

(g) He will come again.

(h) He expects a response from us and that response is in repentance, faith and baptism.

Later came another New Testament scholar, Michael Green who wrote *Evangelism in the Early Church*[4]. He said that although all Dodd's points were right, the gospel could not be captured in a series of statements like that. It was much more alive and flexible than a few facts held in the head. Michael Green's presentation of the good news preached by the first Apostles might be summed up as:

(a) They proclaimed a Person.

(b) They promised gifts to those who believed – the forgiveness of sins and the Holy Spirit.

(c) They preached for a response – repentance, faith and baptism.

Let us take a look at those points.

They proclaimed a Person

Their message was plainly and unapologetically centred in Jesus Christ with its focus on His death and resurrection.[5] Jesus is the centre of the New Testament. Every part of it is about Him. Paul may at one time stress His death (1 Cor. 1: 21) and another time His resurrection (1 Cor. 15: 14) but always the whole Christ is centre and is preached (2 Cor. 4: 5). 'The Good News is about God's Son' (Rom. 1: 3 and 9). 'God has given us eternal life and this life is in His Son' says John (1 John 5: 11).

When Philip was sent by God away from the revival in Samaria to go down towards Gaza (Acts 8) he met the Ethiopian treasury official reading from a scroll part of the book of Isaiah.

'Do you understand what you are reading?' asked Philip.

'How can I,' replied the official, 'unless someone explains it to me?'

And, we are told, Philip began at that very passage 'and preached to him Jesus'. He must have said much more because a few minutes later the Ethiopian is asking to be baptised. But as far as Luke is concerned (Luke is the author of the book of Acts) the whole gospel can be summed up in one word – Jesus.

We were, some time back, conducting a teaching

weekend in a Norfolk village. One older man came and told us his story. Up to the age of fifty-five he had been in the British navy. He was a loner and cared nothing about God. But he had a dream in his heart that by fifty-five – retirement age – he could save up enough money to buy a cottage with a beautiful garden in some lovely village.

He did. He moved in, closed the door and said, 'The rest of you can blow yourselves up if you like. I am going to look after number one now and enjoy life'.

For a little time all went well. Then he fell ill. He was furious with the illness, furious with everything and everybody and furious with whatever gods there might be. He had to go to the doctor, who gave him a prescription. There was only one chemist's shop in the village and when he entered there was a middle-aged lady behind the counter who gave him a lovely smile and said, 'You don't look very happy'.

'No,' he said, 'and neither would you if you felt as bad as I do' and in another minute he was telling her about his dream and all his saving.

'Well,' said the lady, 'at one time I felt as bad about life as you do but my life has been completely changed'.

'Marvellous,' replied the man 'give me a bottle or packet of it, whatever it is'.

'It doesn't come in a bottle or packet,' she said. 'It was Jesus Christ. He changed my life'.

The man had no time for that kind of thing. He gave her a glare and sat down to wait for his prescription. The trouble was that he had to keep on going to the doctor and every time he did he got a prescription. Only one chemist's shop in the village! Every time he went the lady smiled at him but (wise woman) said no more. And every time he glared at her and sat to wait for his prescription. The time came when he had to have a very serious operation. When he came round from the anaesthetic he felt dreadful and thought to himself, 'I'd rather be dead'. Just at that moment the smiling face of the lady came into his mind and he heard again the words 'It was Jesus Christ. He changed my life'.

He said aloud, 'Jesus Christ, if you are real please come and change my life. I need you desperately'. He said it was as if a great glow came around his bed and he felt a tremendous presence before whom he laid his whole life. 'It was not some *thing*,' he said. 'It was some *One*'. When he told us his story he stood with a great smile on his face, now quite well again and now married to the lady in the chemist's shop!

But I shall never forget his words: 'It was not some *thing*. It was some *One*'. That is the essence of Christianity. It is not a theory or a philosophy. It is not a code of conduct or a striving to live a good life. It is a daily fellowship with the living Christ, knowing Him, loving Him, serving Him. Christianity is Christ.

To be committed to Jesus in trust and obedience is life. Not to know Him, however religious we might be, is to have missed the life of God.

'I am come' said Jesus 'that you might have life and that you might have it abundantly' (John 10: 10).

They promised gifts

After Peter's speech on the day of Pentecost the people were deeply disturbed and asked what they must do. Peter replied, 'Repent and be baptised in the Name of Jesus Christ and you will receive the forgiveness of sins and the gift of the Holy Spirit' (Acts 2: 38).

Let us look at these two gifts promised to those who commit their lives to Jesus.

The forgiveness of sins
Some time ago I was travelling from London up to Bedford on the train. At one stop an Indian gentleman got into the carriage and obviously did not understand that British people just do not speak to each other on

trains, for he began to speak to me! He asked me how far I was going and I told him. He then asked if I would do him a favour and I assured him I would if I could. He told me that he was travelling home to the North of England and that he had been delayed for two hours in London. He asked if I would ring up his wife when I arrived at Bedford and tell her that he was quite alright but would be two hours later than promised in getting home. I assured him I would do that and we got chatting together. When he discovered I was a Christian minister he said he was a hindu.

'That's interesting,' I replied. 'What do hindus believe?' (Not because I didn't know but because hindu belief is very broad and I wanted to know what *he* believed!)

'We believe that God is absolutely just,' he said. 'We believe that you are born many times into this world and live many different lives. And anything you do which is good in one life will be done back to you in another life. And anything you do which is bad in one life will be done back to you in another life. So, when all your lives are lived, all you have done will have been done back to you and God will be seen to be absolutely fair.'

Then he asked, 'What do you believe?'

At that moment I realised that the heart of my faith was in the glorious *unfairness* of God! I had to tell my hindu friend about Jesus. I had to tell him that I had done many bad things in my life but they would not be done back to me because another had already paid the price for them. I was the sinner but I was forgiven and my sins washed clean away. He was the sinless One but in His love and redeeming mercy He died for my sins upon the cross.

When Jesus died (the just for the unjust) he cried aloud one great word (it is translated as three words in English but is one word in Greek) 'Tetelestai'. Our Bibles translate it 'It is finished' (John 19: 30). This is the word that a shopkeeper of that day might have written across a bill which had been paid – 'Paid, done with, finished'. When Jesus died for our sins, He paid the bill for our sins. He set us free. Our sins are forgiven, removed from us as far as the east is from the west. They shall have no more dominion over us. God remembers them no more.

There are some Christians who believe in their head that their sins are forgiven but who still carry a sense of guilt, uncertainty or unworthiness in their daily living.

The story is told of an old lady walking along a country road with a big bundle on her back. A farmer came along in his cart, stopped and gave her a lift. As they went along the farmer saw that the old lady still carried the bundle on her back.

'Put your bundle down, my dear,' he said. 'Give yourself a rest.'

'Oh sir,' she replied, 'it's so good of you to give me a lift. I don't want you to have to carry my bundle as well'! The truth was that the farmer was going to take her to her destination whether she put the bundle down or not. And if we ride with Jesus, in trust and obedience, He will carry us through to all His Father's blessings so we may as well put our burdens down right now at the foot of that cross and leave them there.

None of us are worthy, or ever can be. But Jesus has died for us and we live now not in any righteousness of our own but in His righteousness alone.

The Holy Spirit
God not only deals with our past when we trust in Jesus. He gives us a Companion, Guide and Enabler for the future – the Holy Spirit. It is the Holy Spirit who makes us anew in the first place. It is the Holy Spirit who makes Jesus real to us day by day. It is the Holy Spirit who makes the Bible come alive to us. It is the Holy Spirit who gives us strength to do whatever God wants us to do. It is the Holy Spirit who knits us together with other Christians in the Church to make us the Body of

Christ. It is the Holy Spirit who gives gifts so that all the work God wants done can be done in and through that Body. He is the prime Mover in witness.[6] The Christian is never alone and is never left to his own resources. The Spirit of Jesus lives in him and all the resources of God are his.

They preached for a response

When the Apostles preached they expected the Holy Spirit to be using their witness as a channel through which He would do His own work of challenging and changing lives. They expected a response from those who heard and this response was threefold, in repentance, belief and baptism.

Repentance
By nature we live our own lives in the way we think best. We think 'It is my life. I can do what I like with it'. This is of the essence of sin. For sin is not only what we do or do not do. Fundamentally it is what we are – the very set of our mind and will. It is thinking our own thoughts, running our own ways and planning our own paths as if there were no God – as if our lives belonged to us and not to Him. 'All we, like sheep have gone astray. We have turned, every one, to his own way' (Is. 53: 6).

Repentance is turning our back on self, self's way, self-seeking, self-defence, self-aggrandisement and all self-will. It is agreeing with God that that is wrong and quitting it. It is handing over the control panel in the very deepest depths of our personality and being – the will itself.

Belief

Belief is the other side of the same coin as repentance. In repentance we turn our back on self. In belief we turn towards God. Do you believe in God?

When the New Testament speaks of believing in Jesus it does not simply mean holding an opinion or belief in the head. It means a total committal of our will and being and life into the hands of Jesus in trust and obedience.

The story is told of the famous Blondin that he once announced that he would walk a tightrope across the Niagara Falls, blindfolded and wheeling a wheelbarrow. Great crowds gathered to watch him. Blondin arrived, got the wheel of the barrow onto the rope, was blindfolded and surely and steadily walked across to the other side. The crowds cheered him excitedly. Blondin removed the blindfold and asked, 'Do you believe I can do that again?' Of course. Everyone believed he could do it again. They had no doubt of it. They had seen him do it. 'Very well', said Blondin, 'one of you jump into this barrow and I will wheel you back'.

The crowd stood back in alarm. Only one girl came forward, got into the barrow and was wheeled back by Blondin across the great abyss.

Now do you see the difference? All that crowd believed. But only one girl was willing to commit herself in utter trust into Blondin's hands.

Believing in Jesus is a committal just as adventurous and just as final as that. It is a committal to trust and obey Him first and for ever.

Do you really believe in Jesus?

Baptism

Conversion and baptism are closely knit together in the New Testament. When the people on the day of Pentecost asked, 'What shall we do?' Peter replied, 'Repent and be baptised'. The sacrament of baptism and communion are both an outward acting of what is being done in the heart. It is a language that all ages and all tongues can understand. In baptism we say 'Jesus died for me. I accept His death as my own and die with Him. Jesus rose for me. I accept His risen life into myself and rise with Him'. So the candidate is 'buried with Christ in baptism and risen with Him into a new life' (Rom. 6: 3–4). This is what baptism by immersion symbolises. Baptism takes the life and work and Spirit of Jesus into my life now.

During the Second World War I served as a night fighter pilot. At one time our squadron was stationed in Italy and intelligence services reported that the next day at dusk a great column of enemy transport would be travelling down the Jugoslav coast carrying important military equipment. Nine crews (two in each crew) were briefed the next day and toward evening we set off across the Adriatic Sea, flying close to the water so that the enemy radar would not pick us up.

When we got to the Jugoslav coast we lifted over the tree tops and there was the long road full of lorries with their equipment aboard. The drivers very wisely abandoned their lorries and got into the woods and we peeled off, one after the other, and straffed the transport. I was the fourth to do so. By then the Germans had managed to get one 20mm gun firing and as I turned at the end of my run my aircraft was hit right across the starboard wing. Looking at it I could see pieces missing and the wheel flapping in the wind. By this time it was fairly dark but one of our aircraft passed in front of me and I recognised him. I radioed him – 'Robbie, I'm in trouble. Hang on to me, will you?' He came and flew in formation with me and we headed back across the Adriatic Sea.

About halfway back my starboard engine caught on fire. I pulled the lever to let the canopy (the roof of the cabin) go and we released our safety straps preparatory to bailing out. But then I realised that we hadn't the height to bale out so I set myself to land in the sea.

By this time it was pitch black with heavy cloud overhead and nothing visible below. Fortunately we had a radio-altimeter and I 'landed' by this alone. I watched it go down from fifty feet to thirty, twenty then ten and just held everything steady and waited for it. A Mosquito aircraft lands at 130 miles an hour and hitting the sea at that speed is like hitting a brick wall. There was a colossal crash and everything went black. I was quite sure that I was dead. Then two things happened in my mind.

First I saw my family -- father, mother, sister and two brothers, lined up as though they were going to have a photograph taken. (I did not know Molly then.) A feeling of sorrow took hold of me that I should not see them again in this world.

But as I looked with sadness on them, from way beyond came what first appeared to be a light. As it came closer it was not a light but a shining glory. I knew then that it was Jesus and as He came closer there streamed from Him a love so humble as to be awe-ful and a mercy that filled my whole being. I just wanted to fall before Him and worship and adore Him.

He came so close that I expected, despite the brightness of the glory, to see His face. But then He began to go away again. My soul cried 'Lord, why?' But a few moments later I broke the surface of the sea to find my observer swimming around near me. We managed to get my dinghy (made for one) blown up, clambered in and sat there for four-and-a-half hours, every wave lapping over the side, waiting for the Air-Sea rescue boat to pick us up.

But those four and half hours went like four and half seconds. Two things held my mind. One was that all the things we work and strive for in this world finally crumble and come to dust. The other was that in the end it is Him, and Him alone, with whom we have to do. There is no other. He and He alone is the source, meaning and the goal of life in all things and at every point.

There is no other Good News but Him.

Group exercises

1. What particular need in your life brought you to think about commitment to Jesus and what aspect of the gospel answered that need for you? Each answer in turn.

2. The felt need in the early days was for hope greater than death and the early Church came preaching the resurrection. In the Middle Ages the fear was of guilt and there came the Reformers preaching justification by grace through faith. What is the great felt need today and what is the 'cutting edge' of the gospel which matches it?

3. If it was suddenly 'proved' that Jesus Christ never lived at all, would we still have any Good News to offer? If so say why.

4. Suppose you have just met someone who has told you he is a Christian – he hurts no-one, does quite a bit to help others and is as good as anybody else around. Write down shortly what bad news and what Good News you would have to give to him. Each share what you have written.

Part II:

Personal Witness – Methods and Motives

Chapter 4: Why Should I Share My Faith?

There are many Christians who love to dwell on all the promises of God and to receive His blessing and comfort. But they remain babies in Christ and have never grown up to become fellow-workers with God and to feel something of the pain of His love for others.

Jesus warned us clearly that the children of God are those who do the will of God and that judgement comes on those who call Him 'Lord, Lord' but not do what He says.[7]

Why should I share my faith with others?

Because of the nature of God

The mission of the Church arises inevitably from the nature of God. God is not self-absorbed but His Being and life are ever outgoing and outflowing in creation in grace, judgement and love. That outgoing nature is within Himself as a Trinity. His life within His people is therefore outgoing by its very nature. It will always be outflowing and outgoing. For this reason God is seen in the Bible as a sending God. It is there in the story of Abraham, of Moses and of the prophets and through to the New Testament where God sends His Son and His Son sends His people.

The little body of men and women meeting in the upper room of a house in Jerusalem could not settle down comfortably simply to sing hymns, listen to sermons and organise meetings. Had they done so, the Church would have been extinct in half a century. Instead, through them the gospel spread like a living flame over all the then-known world. It had to. It could not be kept in.

No man really knows God without feeling God's love for others. No man is fully one with Christ without his heart beginning to reach out gladly and warmly to bring others to his Lord. When the life of God comes into the life of a man it will begin to overflow.

Because of Jesus (2 Cor. 5: 10–21)

In 2 Corinthians, chapter 5, Paul says we are ambassadors for Christ, or, as J.B. Phillips translates it 'Christ's Special Agents'. In that chapter Paul hints at five reasons why we should share our faith with others.

Because of the judgement of Christ (verses 10–11)
Most people think their life is their own and they can do what they like with it. The gospel reminds us that our lives are not ours, they belong to God. We hold them only as stewards and one day will be called to give account of our stewardship of life and all our gifts and circumstances (Matt 25: 14–30).

Christians, too, need to be reminded that they are given the gospel also in stewardship and one day will give account of their stewardship of the Christian life and faith (1 Cor. 3: 10–15).

Because of the love of Christ (verse 14)
This verse has quite a number of lovely translations in the varying versions of our day – 'the love of God compels us'; 'love holds us in its grip'; 'love leaves us no choice'. What an answer to the question 'Why should I share my faith?'

In his great poem, 'The Everlasting Mercy',[8] John

Masefield tells the story of Saul Kane. Saul Kane was a waster and spent what little money he had on wine, women and song. He was in a pub one night when a Quaker girl came in and began to speak about Jesus. Saul Kane jeered at her. He had no time for that kind of thing. She turned and spoke directly to him and he knew in that moment that he had been confronted not just with the grey eyes of a Quaker girl but by Jesus Himself.

I did not think, I did not strive,
The deep peace burnt my me alive
The bolted door had broken in
I knew that I had done with sin.

He came out of that pub sober to find that not only had he been changed but all things had been changed around him.

The station brook, to my new eyes,
Was bubbling out of Paradise.
The waters rushing from the rain
Were singing Christ has risen again.
I thought all earthly creatures knelt
From rapture of the joy I felt.

What amazed him most was that he – Saul Kane, who never cared a fig for anyone – could not now look upon anyone without loving them.

I felt that Christ had given me birth
To brother every soul on earth.

When the love of Jesus enters a life it not only begins to open that life to warmth, humanity and fulness but it also begin to overflow in caring compassion.

But what if we are Christians who have fallen into the religious mould and have never grown into lively love? The story of Florence Allshorn is of help here.[9] She went out as a missionary to Uganda full of enthusiasm to teach natives about Jesus. When she arrived she found a mission station broken up by bad relationships and an older woman in charge who had grown ill and nervy and with dreadful fits of temper. Of that time she wrote:

'I was young and I was the eighth youngster who had been sent, none of whom had lasted more than two years. I went down to seven stone and my spirit and soul wilted to the same degree. Then one day an old African matron came to me when I was sitting on the verandah crying my eyes out. She sat at my feet and after a time she said, "I have been on this station for fifteen years and I have seen you come out, all of you saying you have brought to us a Saviour, but I have never seen this situation saved yet". It brought me to my senses with a bang. I was the problem for myself. I knew enough of Jesus Christ to know that the enemy was the one to be loved . . . and I prayed . . . that this same love might be in me, and I prayed as I have never prayed in my life for that one thing. Slowly things rightened. Whereas before she had been going about upsetting everybody with long deep dreadful moods, and I had been going into my school depressed and lifeless, both of us found our way to lighten each other. She had a great generosity and I must have been a cruel burden to her, worn out as she was. But I did see that as we two drew together in a new relation the whole character of the work on the station altered. . . . Gradually the whole atmosphere of the place altered. The children felt it and began to share in it, and to do little brave unselfish things they had never done before'.

A whole situation changed when a slip of a girl gave in, let the love of Jesus fill her heart and be expressed in her life.

Because of the purpose of Christ (verse 15)
There are some Christians who never grow to maturity because they have mistaken the purpose of God in their lives. God's prime purpose is not to make us happy.

Sometimes we preachers have misled people by suggesting that if they give their lives to Jesus He will give them joy, peace and blessing – and people come for the gifts and not the giver. God's prime purpose in our lives is not to make us happy but to make us like Jesus: 'that we might be conformed to the image of His Son' (Rom. 8: 29). And that can sometimes be a painful process as God in His Fatherly care has to deal with our lives and does not tolerate anything that is not for His beautiful purpose in us. We sometimes come to God in the same spirit that we go to the dentist, saying 'Please can you take away the pain from this tooth of mine without having to drill or take out the tooth'!

Jesus died that those who live (that is us) 'should no longer live for themselves but only for Him who died for them and is raised to life'. You will notice again and again in the New Testament that the way of discipleship is the way of Christ-likeness (1 John 2: 6). We are commanded to forgive because He has forgiven us (Col. 3: 13) and to love because He has loved us (1 John 4: 11).

And as the Father sent Jesus, so He sends us.

Because of the power of Jesus (verse 17)
'If anyone is in Christ there is a new creation'.

After one conference a married couple in their late twenties came and shared their story. The husband had been on hard drugs and was one day hitching a lift to town to get some more. A girl stopped, gave him a lift and as they went she began to speak to him about Jesus. He was annoyed and stopped her. The next Sunday morning she was on the steps of her church building when she saw him passing. She ran over, took him by the arm and said, 'This is our church. Will you come in?' He was in a daze of drugs at the time and allowed her to lead him into the building. The service made no impression on him at all but afterwards, in the large vestibule, he was surrounded by a group of young Christians, roughly the same age as himself. Through the haze of his mind he was aware that the faces surrounding him were full of joy and love and this he could not understand. 'Surely,' he thought, 'they can see I'm a junkie and they are religious people. They ought not to be looking at me like that'.

Two of them took him to their home and gave him lunch, and during the afternoon he sobered up a bit. And that group of young Christians stood by him week after week while he went through the trauma of giving up drugs. But finally he was free of drugs and committed his life to Jesus. He then wrote to his wife (who had left him), telling his story and asking her to return to him. She got the letter, read it, and thought 'Four times before he has promised that he has given up drugs. Four times I have been back to him but it has never been different. I am not going back a fifth time'. But he kept writing – and his letters were different and in the end she went back to see what had happened. She found her husband a changed man and found herself surrounded by the group of loving young Christians. It was not long before she committed her life to Jesus. And there they stood, hand in hand, transformed people with a transformed marriage.

If Jesus can do things like that, how can I not tell others of Him?

In one of our churches we had a lady of seventy-two who came regularly every Sunday morning. She hated it but she had to come because her mother insisted. Her mother was ninety-four! The old lady was an invalid and had to be pushed to church every Sunday morning in an invalid-chair and her daughter had to sit beside her.

The daughter was the most miserable lady we have ever met. She was one of the kind of whom it is said 'She is never happy unless she is miserable'. We visited her, talked to her and prayed for her but it seemed to make no difference at all. But then her mother died. She had hated looking after her old mother but it had been her whole life and now she found a total emptiness. She had nothing to live for.

She got to the end of her tether and one day knelt down and said, 'Jesus, if you care for me at all despite all I've done, please come into my life and take it over. I need your forgiveness and I need your Spirit'. And Jesus took over her life, gave her face a big tea-pot smile and gave her a work to do in loving and serving others. Today she is a joy to meet.

If Jesus can do things like that, how can I not tell others of Him?

Because of the command of Christ (verse 19)
'He has entrusted to us this message.' Before Jesus went from our sight, He commanded His disciples, on the ground of His Lordship, to go into all the world to make disciples of all peoples. He didn't say 'Go if you happen to have a spare afternoon' or 'if you feel you might be good at it'. He simply said 'Go' and that is a command of the Lord.

Were you ever entrusted with a message as a child? Do you remember how you went out and had to pass the toy-shop window? You pressed your nose against the glass and went round all the toys in turn, playing with each one in your imagination. Then you remembered the message and hurried on. But round the corner you met some friends and stayed to play with them. You had a great time until you heard a clock strike five and realised it was tea time. You ran home and the first words your mother said were 'Did you deliver the message?'

'Oh, no, mum, I forgot'.

'Then go and do it. There will be no tea for you until you deliver the message'.

And what if the first words of Jesus when you arrive in heaven at last are 'Did you deliver the message?' Remember, 'He has entrusted to us a message'.

Because of the Holy Spirit

The Holy Spirit is the Inspirer, the Life and the Guide in witness to Jesus. In John chapter 20 the risen Jesus appears to His disciples and says to them: ' "As the Father has sent me, so do I send you" ' and 'He breathed on them and said, "Receive the Holy Spirit" '.

Again in Acts 1: 8 Jesus, just before His ascension said to His disciples, 'When the Holy Spirit comes upon you, you will be filled with power, and you will be witnesses for me in Jerusalem, in all Judea and Samaria and away to the ends of the earth.' Further Luke describes this promise of Jesus to His disciples as 'instructions given through the Holy Spirit' (Acts 1: 2).

The Spirit of Jesus lives in the believer giving him the compassion and love of Jesus (2 Cor. 5: 14, Rom. 5: 8) and both in and through the believer the Spirit testifies of Jesus (John 15: 26–27 and 16: 14).

Not only the Acts of the Apostles but the whole movement of New Testament Christianity is the movement of the Holy Spirit through the people of Jesus. The Holy Spirit is the Spirit of communication and without Him our words and acts are empty.

Molly, after her conversion, speaks of coming to read the Bible again 'and it was as if a torch was shining on the words and through them God was speaking to me'. It is the Holy Spirit who inspires (sometimes compels) us to speak and it is the Holy Spirit who enables others to see and hear God in our witness. Without the Holy Spirit evangelism is no longer an overflow of the life of Jesus within us but becomes mere scalp-hunting or a seeking for church growth for our own glory. It becomes not a genuine sharing in love but an attempt to manipulate in which the other becomes not more free to choose but less free. Without the Holy Spirit the whole Christian life falls into the traps of legalism, private pietism or human activism and all of them ways of escaping encounter with the living God. Mission without the

Spirit of Jesus is only an ugly caricature seeking only our own self-satisfaction or aggrandisement. But where the Spirit of Jesus is, inevitably and genuinely, there is mission. The two are closely linked in the New Testament and in Christian experience.

Group exercises

1. What do you think was the strongest motive for witness in the New Testament Church?

2. Which motive touches your own heart most? Each share in turn.

3. What main hindrances to witness do you experience? Each share in turn.

4. Make a list of the hindrances. How many are within ourselves and how many outside ourselves? What can we do to increase our motivation?

Chapter 5: Where Can We Share and Who Can Share?

These questions can be answered simply and immediately. Anyone who has a 'today' experience of the Lord Jesus, whether they are nine or ninety-nine, a marathon runner or housebound, can share their experience with anyone they meet. The important proviso is that they *have* a 'today' experience of Jesus. God does not give everyone the gift of an evangelist but He has given us all the ability to communicate. If we have a real experience of the Lord Jesus living in our lives by the power of His Holy Spirit, not only should we be able to share but we are being disobedient to Him if we do not.

In Acts 8: 4 we read that everywhere the early Christians went they preached the gospel. They were ordinary people: few were well educated and none trained evangelists and they were persecuted and scattered because they were Christians. In this modern era we have greater opportunities.

Where can we share?

1. In Church life
The reason many of us find it embarrassing and difficult to share our Christian experience with non-Christians is that we seldom talk about what God is doing in our lives to *church* friends. If we have not a 'today' experience of Jesus Christ and all the testimony we have is how we became a Christian years ago, perhaps we need to get

down on our knees in repentance and ask God to show us what is missing in our life today. We are all very good at speaking about the weather, our aches and pains, the state of the world and the church organisations but not so good at talking about the Lord. Lewis is usually preaching at a different church each Sunday and I travel with him. He is never late – in fact if we leave on time for a trip he considers we are ten minutes late! When we arrive for the service Lewis goes into the vestry and I find a seat fairly near the front of the church as I usually do the reading. During the twenty minutes or so before the service I learn a tremendous amount about the people gathering behind me: Mrs so-and-so is in hospital; another lady has had a fall; someone's children have measles, and so on. Seldom do I hear of blessings someone has received, of prayers being answered or how a Christian led someone to the Lord. Sadly the Lord's name is rarely mentioned. During the service we may sing, 'Take my lips and let them be, filled with messages for thee,' but as soon as the service is over we go back to our chit-chat. It is not necessarily unkind gossip and we do need to share news of the fellowship but would it not be wonderful if we talked about what God had done for us during the service? If we are sufficiently sensitive to discern when the person we are speaking to has not committed their life to Christ there is the opportunity to ask, 'Was the sermon a help to you?' or 'Was there anything you did not understand in the service?' Be ready to talk naturally about the Lord and sensitive enough to know when to stop.

There are many opportunities too during our weekly organisations to share the Lord Jesus. If we have a 'today' experience of Him let us use these opportunities well. There may, for instance, be elderly people coming to church luncheon clubs, some of whom are back on church premises after many years away. We have a God-given responsibility to share the answer to life and death. If the Christians who run the clubs talk naturally about the Lord Jesus and show His love in other ways – while praying regularly for the elderly folk – miracles can happen. One of the liveliest eighty-year-olds we have met was in a church in the south of England. She greeted us with, 'I am Hallelujah Jessie!' She was bubbling over with the joy of the Lord. For many years she had been a regular attender at the church but as she put it, 'I've only just understood what the gospel is all about. I've found Jesus and He has found me!' At her recent baptism, as she came up out of the water she said, 'Hallelujah!' and now everyone calls her – to her great delight – Hallelujah Jessie. She was a reminder that there can be many people in our churches who have been listening to the gospel for many years but have never made their own personal commitment to Christ, claiming God's forgiveness and a new life in Jesus. When challenged as to whether they are a Christian sometimes the answer is, 'I hope so'. Never just leave them there. God may be wanting you to show them how they can be sure. If they are married say to them, 'Are you married?' then 'How do you know you are married?' Of course we know. We do not say, 'I hope so'. Not only was there the first commitment on our wedding day but for some of us many years of a close relationship. I vividly remember using this illustration in a coffee morning among young wives, the majority of whom were not Christians, and seeing their faces light up as they had realised for the first time what commitment to Christ meant.

Every fringe member of our fellowship, and all contacts who are not committed Christians, should be on a prayer list of a church member or prayer triplet so that the Holy Spirit is working in lives all the time, bringing the uncommitted nearer to Christ. When we pray for them God increases our love for them and should make us sensitive and aware of the time to speak.

Our last pastorate was in a large council estate near Birmingham. One Sunday morning a young man called Eric came to our service. He did not normally go to church. None of his family did, but during the previous week he had had an accident on his motorbike. This made him wonder what would have happened to him if he had been killed, and made him think about God. Among the notices on the leaflet Eric was given when he came to church was one for a house group meeting that week in a home in the road in which he lived. This attracted his eye, so on Wednesday evening he went to the house group which had recently been started for new Christians. Eric sat very quietly listening to these very new Christians, most from non-Church backgrounds, talking with great excitement about what Jesus was doing in their lives, full of joy at prayers being answered and the Bible coming alive to them. Eric said very little but of course they were asking lots of questions too, some of those he wanted answered. Before this series of classes was finished Eric had committed his life to the Lord. Soon his wife became interested, began to ask questions and she became a radiant Christian. The next house group began in their home!

2. At home

A few years ago Lewis was visiting one of our church members – a married girl in her thirties. She was complaining that she could not do any Christian service because she had small children. Her husband had a responsible job which often took him away from home so she could not get involved in any church organisations. Lewis had lovingly to point out that she had her own private mission field. She had the responsibility of seeing her husband cared for and ministered to so that he (also a Christian) could go off happily each day to do the work that was his Christian vocation. Her children depended on her loving concern twenty-four hours of every day. They needed to grow up feeling secure in a happy and encouraging Christian atmosphere that would enable them to cope with the harshness of the world later. Also, because of the woman she was, neighbours were often in for a chat or bringing their problems. All this was first class Christian service but she had never seen it so. We must seriously consider the Christian teaching we give that makes church members think the only service they can give to the Lord is on church premises or in church organisations. There are unique opportunities of sharing our experience of Christ in our homes. Let us look further at some of them:

(a) *The Christian family* In Deuteronomy 4: 9 and 6: 6 to 7 the Israelites were given specific instructions on how they should teach God's law in the home. They were told not to forget the laws and to tell them to their children and their grandchildren at different times of the day.

Children are the easiest people to talk to about God, especially when they are young. They are always asking questions. We must always answer them in a way which they can understand at their age. Never put them off but try honestly to find an answer if one can be found. As for every age, when we pray for people God is going to give us opportunities to talk about Him to prepared hearts.

When non-Christian friends or family visit a home where Christ is talked about naturally because He is at the centre of the home, it is easy for them to ask questions too.

The parents must have their own daily experience of Jesus Christ and find time together to read and pray and share. Then God can make their home a mission base He can use.

(b) *Non-Christian partners* Of course all we have said about a Christian home cannot be the same if one of the partners is not a committed Christian. This does not make the responsibility less for the one who is. He or she has to represent Christ to the family on their own. There will always be opportunities to share when the Christian acts in a way which is loving, sensitive and prayerful. Never push your opinions or beliefs on your partner but always be sensitive to opportunities.

The non-Christian husband of a church member in the west of England rang the minister one day. 'What have you done to my wife?' he demanded. Somewhat taken aback the minister said, 'What do you mean?' The husband said, 'My wife is cooking all my favourite meals, waves me off at the door when I go to work and is waiting for me when I return with my slippers warmed. She seems really to care about me. If this is what being a Christian is all about I am interested'. This kind of Christianity is infectious.

(c) Hospitality If all your family are Christians, God has given you the opportunity of hospitality and if one of you likes cooking consider prayerfully how God can use your home.

A few years ago when we had recently moved to a new part of the country a fellow minister and his wife asked us to an evening meal just before Christmas. We thought we were the only ones to be invited. When we arrived we found that two other couples, neighbours of our host, had also been invited. Lewis was introduced just as a friend and everyone began very naturally to talk about their work. They were as interested in what Lewis did as we were in hearing about their jobs. As Lewis was travelling the country teaching Christians how to share the faith it was easy and natural to explain the gospel.

During the war I was in the WAAF. After many years in the north of England I was posted to a bomber station near Cambridge. I met a girl called Joan who invited me to go with her to a little church seven miles away. She said that any forces folks who went were invited to the home of the lay pastor and his wife. When living away from home, especially on an RAF camp it was always good to have a meal in homely surroundings, so I appreciated being invited myself. I shall never forget my first visit to that home, although I remember little of the church service. Mr Burton was a farm labourer and their home was humble, but they certainly had the gift of hospitality and *they loved the Lord*. No matter how many airmen and WAAF came from the RAF stations nearby there was always enough simple food. The standard menu was boiled eggs, bread and butter and junket (a sweet made just with milk and rennet) – all things they could produce from the farm in spite of rationing. But what I shall never forget was Mr and Mrs Burton themselves. Before we all left to cycle to our various stations Mr Burton read some verses from the Bible and in his lovely Cambridgeshire accent shared what God was saying to him through them. Others also spoke about what God was doing in their lives at that time. I had always believed in God, had been brought up to say my prayers, go to church and read my Bible, but as I went regularly with Joan to that Christian fellowship and to Mr and Mrs Burton's home I began to realise I did not know Jesus like the folk there. One day Joan said to me as we were cycling back to camp, 'You don't say very much, Molly'. I realised I had not much to say. My experience until then had been religion, church and 'doing things' and I had quite a lot of head knowledge of God and Jesus Christ but no 'today' experience of Him.

One day at a gospel service I was really challenged by God. I just said to God, 'I don't know what all these years of church-going have been about, but I want to know you personally. Please come into my life and give me a real experience of you'. And He did. He came into my life in a wonderful way making the Bible, some of which I knew by heart, really come alive as if a torch shone on it and I understood for the first time. And prayer became real conversation and fellowship with the Lord Jesus. I shall never cease to thank God for Mr and Mrs Burton and their loving Christian hospitality. They shared what they had and the Lord multiplied it.

3. Among friends and neighbours

In our travels I met two ladies who spoke about their neighbours. One said she realised she had not seen her neighbour for a while, so she knocked on her door. She discovered that the neighbour had been ill for three weeks. 'Why didn't you let me know?' the Christian said, 'I would have come and helped'. The neighbour replied, 'I know you are always so busy at the church I didn't want to bother you'. What a picture of a Christian – one who is too busy in a church building to be a true neighbour!

The other lady told of new neighbours recently moved in next door. She said, 'I did a very stupid thing. As soon as we met I asked the lady to come to church with me. She wasn't a bit interested and now she avoids me. If I go into our garden and she is in hers she hurries indoors to avoid speaking. I realise I should have found out more about her and built up a relationship before talking about church'.

There are many people who are not interested in the Church or its organisations but they are interested in God and believe in Him and few are uninterested in Jesus. If we want to win our neighbours for the Lord we must first pray for them and care about them. Then when God is working in their lives He will give us His own opportunity to share what we know of Him working in our lives. Many of us, like these ladies, have made mistakes in our approach but God will forgive them and can teach us something through them.

4. While shopping

The Christian life is an adventure which can be very exciting if we begin every day by asking God to give us a divine appointment with someone.

One day I was in a market buying eggs. The man selling them swore using the name of Jesus. I found myself saying, 'Please don't do that. Jesus is a friend of mine'. He looked rather surprised then apologised. He wasn't rude or unpleasant. Many times I have missed opportunities like that so when this happened I thanked God for giving me the words to say and have prayed for that man many times since. God does not expect us to talk about the complete gospel every time we share our faith, but He expects us to be faithful in using the opportunities He gives us.

Some months ago we were staying with a lady who told us a wonderful story. One day she was walking into town to do some shopping. All the time the phrase, 'Do you understand what you are reading?' (Acts 8: 30) kept coming into her mind. She could not understand why. She knew the story of Philip and the Ethiopian of course but had not read it recently. She arrived at the High Street and was just going into a store when she noticed a lorry parked at the kerb. The driver was in the cab reading a Bible! Before she realised what she was doing she tapped on the window and said, 'Do you understand what you are reading?' He wound down his window and answered, 'No, I don't. My life is in a mess and I am trying to find God. Can you help me?' So just like Philip (Acts 8: 26–35) she climbed into the cab and heard about a broken marriage and a shattered life. That driver found God that day.

God could use that woman because first of all she knew the Bible well enough for Him to remind her of those words He wanted her to use at that time. She was also sensitive to God's voice and obedient when He gave her the opportunity to share what she knew of Him.

Another exciting modern miracle happened to the son of a Baptist minister friend of ours – a modern prodigal who left home and the family lost touch with him for a while. One day he arrived home an excited radiant Christian. God had used a very ordinary elderly lady to answer the parents' prayers. The lad was in a town a long way from home sitting on a bench looking lost, hungry and rather dirty. This lady, doing her shopping, noticed him and felt a Christian concern, so went to speak to him.

He told her he was a long way from home and had not any money and did not know what to do. She prayed quickly in her heart, then asked him if he would like to come home with her. He went. She gave him a good meal, a bath, some clean clothes *and* talked to him about the Lord Jesus. Of course he knew *about* Him, but had never found Him for himself. That old lady had the joy of leading him to the Saviour.

Just think of the many excuses that lady could have used for leaving that young man where he was: She was elderly, probably coping on a pension, and she lived alone. She knew nothing about the lad and he did not look very respectable. Human reasoning would say she had done a dangerous thing. But perhaps she began her day with a prayer that God would give her something to do for Him.

5. At work

Lewis has never forgotten a man who worked in the same office as he did many years ago. One day he visited this man – a Christian – in his home. On his wall was a picture of every member of the office, with each name and a few details about each. On a separate square was a picture of the boss with his name and a few words. That Christian man prayed for every person in turn whose lives he touched at work every day. God knows the difference this made to the office atmosphere.

So often Christian or 'religious' people at work are identified by a negative image – they *do not* do this or that. Let us be positive Christians; positively happy, positive about what we believe and who we believe and with absolute assurance for the future in this uncertain world, and not just seen as those who do not swear, smoke or gamble. If we are praying regularly for the people we work with, especially the most difficult ones, God will give us an opportunity to share our faith with them. When that comes do not waste the firm's time; say a word that is necessary to show you are not avoiding the issue, then arrange to have your coffee break or lunch with them. And do not ask them to come to church straight away. It is not going to church that makes our life different but having a living Saviour in control of our life.

Do be interested in those you work with. If you regularly pray for them God will help you to care naturally about them. Find out their interests and watch the same programmes on TV (selectively!) so you have a basis for discussion.

Today many more people than we realise are interested in God. Some are clever and will produce the most outrageous arguments against Christianity. Be sensitive to know when someone *really* wants to have an answer or whether they just enjoy an argument. Do not win the argument and lose the person but do know the facts you need to know. Read the daily papers, and if you can, find out the truth of things you are told. Above all, know what you believe and, although you may be asked questions you cannot answer, never be frightened to say you do not know. If it is a serious question that can be answered promise to find out. You can always say, 'I don't know that but I can tell you what I do know!'

Who can share?

At the beginning of this chapter I said that *anyone* who has a 'today' experience of Jesus can share what they know of Him. In Jim Peterson's book *Evangelism as a Lifestyle*[10] he tells how his thirteen year old son, Todd, came to him one day and asked him how he could be a good witness for Jesus. His sister was always talking to her friends about Christ and Todd felt he was not such a good Christian as she was. Remembering how difficult he had found it as a teenager Jim Peterson suggested that Todd should not worry too much about words but he should begin by trying to be a peacemaker among his friends. That would be doing what God wanted in that situation. A few weeks later Todd fell out with his friend from next door and they stopped spending time together. Todd was upset and talked it over with his father. They read together from Romans 12: 17,18, 'Do not repay anyone evil for evil. Be careful to do what is right in the eyes of everybody. If it is possible as far as depends on you, live at peace with everyone'. Todd visited the other boy and they were friends again. Not long after this the mother of the boy called saying how impressed the family were by Todd's attitude. They felt their neighbours had something they would like – and they became Christians.

When we began a church in a large overspill estate nine miles from Birmingham we visited the Senior Citizens Club regularly. We chatted to the folk then said a prayer at the end of the afternoon. Few of these folk had any church connections but there was always absolute silence during the prayers, a fervent 'Amen' at the end and many thanked us afterwards. We met Maud there. She was seventy and a pale and very unhappy lady. For many years she had lived with her married daughter and her family in the centre of Birmingham. Now they had been rehoused in this vast estate but could not be given a house large enough for Maud to live with them. She had a bungalow just opposite, but Maud did not like living alone and she hated being in her hew home. We visited her and she began to come to our Sunday service. One day she shared with us that as a young girl, from a completely non-Christian background she had felt a real desire to know about God and began to attend the Methodist Central Hall in Birmingham. Jesus became very real to her then but later she married a man who was not interested at all and she had not been to church since. Now in a Christian fellowship again Maud became a changed person. Instead of being a miserable lady her face shone and many times she thanked God for her lovely home on her own where she could pray and read her Bible just whenever she wanted.

Soon after this we were having a training day for Christians to learn how to share their faith. Maud said, 'I would love to come on Saturday but I can't.' I said, 'Why can't you?'. Maud answered, 'You know I am over seventy and I am so shy, I find it difficult to talk with people I don't know'. I encouraged her to come by saying I would sit beside her and we would share the day together.

The first part of the day we learned how to articulate our faith, explaining in every day language how we became Christians and what difference Christ had made in our lives. In the afternoon we were sent out in twos visiting in the area around the church building. Maud and I were given a block of flats. We went up to the top storey in the lift knocking at doors on the way down. (If you begin at the bottom you are apt to collect children and be a bit like the Pied Piper of Hamelin before you get far!) It was a wonderful experience. We went in fear and trembling but found many people interested and no hostility. One young married woman came to the Lord on her doorstep and became a lively member of the fellowship. Then we visited another woman, a Mrs Jones who had worshipped with us a few times. Maud felt able to share her faith and Mrs Jones also opened her life to Christ before we left. This was a tremendous encouragement to Maud.

The following week I suggested to Maud that we should go back to the flats, visit all the contacts we had made and arrange a Bible study for the new Christians. After praying about this we set off having decided to visit Mrs Jones first. In the lift with us was a young, very pregnant girl who got out with us and went into the flat next to Mrs Jones. Mrs Jones was out, so the pregnant girl kindly invited us in. This young lady, Janet, made us some tea then asked us who we were and what we were doing visiting in the flats. We told her we were Christians and were calling to find people who were interested so that we could share our faith with them.

She looked at us in amazement then said, 'Isn't that extraordinary! Last week I bought a modern translation of the New Testament. I want to find God. Can you help me?'

Janet shared a bit of her life with us. She had been brought up to go to church, had married a lad who was not at all interested, but suddenly Janet felt a real conviction of sin and desperately wanted God's forgiveness. It was not difficult to point her to Jesus and soon the three of us were praying. Janet became a lovely Christian girl and is still praying for her husband.

I shall never forget the joy on Maud's face at seeing these miracles. She said, 'I shall not be frightened to share my faith any more'. Maud would never be a talkative extrovert but in her quiet way she was always ready to tell friends at the Senior Citizens Club, her neighbours and her family the difference God had made in her life. Soon after this her granddaughter became a Christian and this gave Maud much joy.

A few months ago I was in a ladies' toilet when I overheard an excited conversation. One lady was obviously wearing a new coat which was being admired by the other. 'Yes,' said the owner of the coat, 'it is nice. Do you know how much I paid for it? It was only twenty-five pounds. They are twenty pounds more at Marks and Spencers, but this is a "second". I am so excited I tell everyone about it'. Her enthusiasm for her bargain came over in her voice. So as not to forget the actual words I wrote them down – 'I am so excited I tell everyone about it'. Her bargain coat so thrilled her she wanted to tell everyone the good news.

The Good News of the Lord Jesus is life-saving Good News. Shall we ask God to make us so excited about Him that we must share that Good News whenever and wherever He gives us the opportunity?

As Paul says:
'Be wise in the way you act towards those who are not believers, making good use of every opportunity you have.

74

Your speech should always be pleasant and interesting, and you should know how to give the right answer to everyone' (Col, 4: 5,6).

Group exercises

1. Have three minutes' silence while each member of the group estimates quickly how many people they speak to each week who do not know Jesus. Add them all together. How many possibilities every week does this group alone have to speak a word for Jesus?

2. How could we make better (non-pressing but open, loving and honest) use of our contacts?

3. What 'witnesses' have attempted to share their faith with you in the past (including cults) and have been off-putting rather than attractive. Why? Share in turn.

4. Who has influenced you most deeply for Jesus and why? Each share in turn.

Chapter 6: Sharing Through Testimony

At some time in the past you may well have seen a man carrying a placard with a Bible text upon it – usually something fairly grim, such as 'Prepare to meet your God'.

If you have been wise you will have given your attention not to the man and his placard but to the people around. And you will have observed that the effect that the man achieves is to make people feel that Christianity is something 'cranky' and best avoided. The man is doubtless a good Christian brother. He is probably a deeply devoted man and has a good deal more courage than most of us. And yet, despite his intention to turn people towards God, he is in fact sending people further away. Why is that? I think perhaps he has not yet learned the ways of Jesus. Jesus had no great organisation behind Him and no pre-packed message to thrust upon people. He did not come 'shouting, raising His voice or making loud speeches in the streets'. He did not write some great message across the sky or push tracts through people's letter boxes. He 'came and dwelt among us, full of grace and truth' (John 1: 14). He met people naturally and genuinely in the midst of human life and by His attention made people who felt worthless feel of infinite worth. In warm humanity and personal loving contact He became involved with people, willing to give Himself to them and for them. The proclamation of His message was not only in His words but in all that He was and did. Our words will be useless without the same life and Spirit behind and coming through them.

For these reasons the basic method of witness will always be through the daily life of every Christian, loving and befriending others. Test any group of Christians and you will find most have come to Jesus through the help or witness of another caring Christian.

However, although caring for and befriending people are the main ways God uses to draw people closer to himself be careful in case you make them a 'method'! All Christians should have many friendships outside the church as well as in it, the product of a genuinely warm and overflowing heart and not as a means of evangelism. But real friendship means honesty and sharing and will include sharing the deepest and most precious thing we have – our relationship with Jesus.

Let us look, then, at the simplest way of sharing – telling another of what Jesus has done in our lives – giving a testimony.

Why give a testimony?

Let us look at two reasons:

1. People are interested in people.
If I said, for instance, to a congregation, 'Telephone calls in the night are a nuisance' probably most would agree with me but I would get little response or interest. But it would be different if I said, 'An annoying thing happened to me one night. I was in a deep sleep when the telephone rang at two o'clock in the morning. When at last the ringing got through to my brain, I jumped out of bed, sure it must be some dire emergency. I fell downstairs and grabbed the phone and a man said "Is that the Blue Star Garage?" I told him I was not and he asked my number. I gave it to him and he said triumphantly, "That's the Blue Star Garage". I repeated

that I was not a garage and that ours was a private number only to hear his angry voice saying, "Yes, you are the garage but you just don't want to come out". I assured him that I knew less about cars than he did and if I came and tended his car it would undoubtedly be useless for a very long time. He finally rang off but I still hadn't convinced him I was not a garage'.

If I told that story to a congregation I would get an instant and visible response. They would be interested. That is the strength of a testimony. If you give people a piece of information about the Christian faith, they may agree but they will pass on with little concern about it. But when you tell them what happened in your life (simply sharing, not trying to get at them through what you say) the experience lives again in you and communicates in lively fashion to others.

2. *It speaks of life and not of theory.*

A testimony speaks of what has happened to you in the midst of your life and people are left thinking, 'If that happened to that person it is something that could happen to me.' Again it becomes relevant and lively rather than a piece of information which glances off the top of people's heads. Paul told the story of his conversion at least twice (Acts 22 and 26) and those who heard found it powerful and persuasive.

People may have the most wonderful arguments and questions about Christian doctrine and statements but a sharing of what happened to you in your life comes from an angle that bears its own authenticity. With all their arguments you may have to say, 'I am sorry I don't understand your argument but I do know I was blind but now I see' or 'I am sorry I can't answer your question. If it is important to you I will try to find out. In the meantime let me just tell you what happened to me'. That is always living because it is a piece of yourself and your own story you are offering to them and Jesus is livingly present in the offering speaking His own Word through the word you give.

So giving a personal testimony, lovingly and honestly, is a lively and good way of witnessing to Jesus.

What makes a good testimony?

1. It points to Jesus and not to you.
Doubtless you have heard testimonies which leave you amazed at what happened but also leave the impression that the person who gave it is in some way extraordinary. It does not occur to you for a single moment that what happened to them could happen to you.

A testimony should leave people thinking about Jesus, not about you. It should leave them with a wistful wondering: 'Could that be for me too?' It should be a touch of sunshine enticing them to open the windows of their souls to the extraordinary mercy and grace of the Redeemer.

2. It is not complicated with unnecessary detail.
We all know the kind of person who gets sidetracked with irrelevant detail: 'It was on a Wednesday in Easter week . . . No, I believe it was a Tuesday . . . No, it must have been a Wednesday because that's the day the butcher comes. I have a butcher who delivers because I had such a job getting to the shops when I was living in Smith Street. He is such a nice man. Always reminds me of an uncle I used to have . . .' – and so the story goes on from one irrelevancy to another and we never get to know what it was that she was trying to say when she began.

Cut out all unnecessary detail and get down to the simple facts of what happened to you so that people understand it clearly.

At the same time do include relevant detail. Avoid vague phrases like 'He told me about Jesus' or 'I gave my heart to Jesus'. Say what actually came home to you and challenged you and say it simply, clearly and shortly. Say how you gave your life to Jesus: 'I knelt down on my own and said, "Lord Jesus, for what this life of mine is worth I hand it all over to you and to your control. Please, cleanse my life of all that does not please you and fill it with your own Spirit" '. This helps people who are moved by your testimony to have a clear idea of what they can do and say to give their own lives to the Lord. That is relevant detail.

3. It is relevant to the need of your contact.
Choose from your own experience of Jesus those parts of your story which fit the needs of the person you are talking to. A testimony does not always have to be the story of your conversion. I hope that is not the only experience of God you have had! Our experience of Jesus and His loving mercy ought to be a daily one with many incidents of grace within it.

I remember an occasion when I was asked to give my testimony at a big rally. Our son came to me and said, 'Dad, don't tell them what the Lord did for you thirty-seven years ago. Tell them what He has done for you this week'. We should all endeavour to give an up-to-date testimony. If you can't do that, then what happened to you many years ago will not have life and meaning for today.

So, first listen with loving care to the other person. Try to sense and feel their own need. Begin there. It may be that the person you are talking to is feeling lonely. If there is in your experience a time when you felt lonely and Jesus was a tremendous strength and blessing to you then, that is the part of your story you will share. You cannot, of course, match every need with a similar experience of your own. But so often, if you are prepared and pre-prayered, the Lord will lead to you people whose needs you can address.

There is no one who can help a woman recently

widowed like another widow. To anyone else she can say, 'You do not know how I feel'. But to another widow she cannot say that. They share something together.

Do remember that there is no better place to begin than where the other person is. Some tracts assume that everyone begins with a feeling of sin or guilt but that is not always so. In my own case, the felt need in my teens was for some power to unify my life and take it forward in one (and a good) direction. I was very aware of so much striving for good within me and so much potential for evil – all mixed up. It was that awareness of need that made me ready for Jesus to change my life.

I have to confess that I had very little sense of my own sin until I began to know Jesus more closely. It was looking at Him that made me see how far I was from all that He is. But then the sense of sin did not plunge me deeper into self-rejection and alienation. He had come to me, right where I was, and my sense of being far from home brought only growing gratitude and worship that in grace and mercy He had come to lead me back to God.

Different people have different beginnings and different experiences in The Way. These things we can share, gently and honestly, as and when it is helpful to others where they are.

An old preacher, F W Boreham, used to say witnessing was like playing dominoes.[11] The art of the game is first to match your partner's piece. But because your piece has another end to it, in putting it down you change the game.

4. It avoids 'churchy' words.

Often we church people speak in jargon – a language which we understand but others do not. Take, for instance, the word 'converted'. To us it is full of the love and mercy of the Lord Jesus Christ who has changed our lives, their meaning and their direction. To the non-Christian it usually means that we have 'become religious' (from which Lord preserve us) or that we have changed our denomination. It is far better to talk simply of how you discovered Jesus Christ is still alive and active and how He changed your life.

Similarly 'born-again' is becoming more often used but more often misused. It would be better to say, 'It was just as though He made my life all over anew'.

Words like 'justification', 'regeneration', 'sanctific-ation' and phrases like 'washed in the blood of the Lamb' may be meaningful to us but they do need to be turned into more simple language for those not brought up on 'the language of Zion'. It is not enough for us to say things that are good and true if we say them in a language foreign to the other person.

5. It is honest.
Giving your testimony is not only an offering to the person before you. It is an offering to God, that He might use it as a vehicle through which His Holy Spirit might travel to do his own work of confronting and changing people. The Holy Spirit is the Spirit of truth (or of reality) and He cannot use your words if they are not genuine. Do not exaggerate how bad you were before Jesus met you – or how angelic you now are! Tell it how it is and let the emphasis be on Him, His loving mercy and His continuing guidance and care.

We had a friend with quite a good 'conversion story' but she was always petrified at speaking in public. On one occasion we saw her standing white-faced and strained in a Christian meeting telling people how happy the Lord had made her! The 'body language' was in fact more powerful than the verbal message.

Remember that it is not important that the story you share should be dramatic. Not everyone, for example, has a dramatic conversion experience. Some can tell you the date and the hour Jesus changed their lives. Praise God for that. But there are others who cannot point to any particular incident or moment. They only know that

Jesus has come into their lives, is a daily reality to them and is shaping their lives into His own likeness. Jesus is alive to them now and that is all that matters. There are people they can help in personal sharing that a dramatic testimony might leave with a 'not-for-me' feeling.

6. *Sometimes it includes a text.*
If there is a text – a short sentence or phrase from the Bible – that was a great help to you in the particular piece of your story you are sharing, then give that text to the person you are talking to. If you are relating your own experience to their need, the text is likely to be a help to them too. If you carry copies of a gospel with you which contains the text, open it, talk about it, underline it and hand over the gospel when you go.

How to share your testimony

1. *Ask God for a holy boldness.*
We say 'holy boldness' because there is an unholy boldness. We do not want to go out 'thrusting religion down people's throats' without sensitivity or wisdom. That puts others off – and rightly so. But most of us fail on the other side and are frightened at the idea of sharing our faith and of what people might say if we do.

We need to surrender our fears to Jesus and ask Him for freedom to be ourselves, to share very simply what we have (and not what we do not have) and to offer it to others and to God. Our part is simply to share and to leave the rest to God.

And do remember that 'success' in spiritual terms may not be in numbers coming to Christ, but in doing and being what Jesus asks you to do and be just when He asks you. So ask God for a relaxed, open, loving spirit – ask Him for His Holy Spirit, the Spirit of Jesus. That is not something you can put on for the occasion. It is God's gift to those who trust and obey.

2. *Look at the person you are talking with.*

There is nothing worse, when talking with people, than sitting, not listening to what they say but just waiting to get your 'God bit' in. God will do His own bit if we make the bridge of loving relationship over which He comes.

Our first need is to give our attention to the one we are talking with; listening with care and interest. You will then speak relevantly when you do speak and the other will know you speak because you care about them.

I am a great reader and in a spare five minutes I will put my head into a book. Maybe during an evening I will begin to read and then Molly will say something to me. I murmur 'Yes, dear' but my mind is still in my book. A line or two further on and she will speak again and I have a choice to make – my wife or my book! The only thing to do is to put my book down, to turn toward her and give her my attention. To love my wife means to give her myself.

In witness, not only the words we say but what we are and the attitude others discern in us are centrally important. We are to love people and that means giving them our selves, our time, our attention and our interest.

Parents often discover this. They work hard to give their children things, only to discover that their children do not want things. What they want is the parents themselves, the relationships of love. They want you, your time, your caring, your listening, your attention. Perhaps that is what we all want deep down – someone else to give us time, attention and loving care – to give us of themselves.

So look at the person you are talking with – really look at them, see them, love them, offer them your time, your attention and your care. Offer them yourself.

3. *Be happy.*

Even if your words are neither clever nor conclusive, let the joy of the Lord be communicated through you.

There was one girl, trained in our classes in visitation, who went out on her first doorstep and, at her own request, went on her own. She was quite frightened and would have been a lot more frightened had she known whose doorstep she stood upon. The man of that house had been there only two weeks and was already known in the neighbourhood for his drinking capacity and his temper. When he fell out with his wife the whole row shook and all the neighbours knew about it. Our girl knocked. The door opened and there was Len looking down at her. The girl was so frightened that she forgot all her opening sentences and all she had been taught to show interest in others. After an embarrassed pause she blurted out, 'I've come to share my faith with you'.

Len was so surprised he simply blinked and grunted and the girl took this as permission to continue! She began to tell him what Jesus meant to her and had done in her life and as she told her story she relived it and her face glowed. All the fear went and was replaced by joy.

When she completed her story she was lost for words again and simply looked at Len for some kind of response. He grunted again and closed the door! The girl came back discouraged and said, 'I've made an awful mess of my first visit'. But Len went down the corridor into the kitchen and said to his wife, 'There was a girl on our doorstep talking about Jesus Christ'. His wife replied, 'Oh yes' and carried on getting the meal. 'But,' continued Len, 'she was so happy'.

Len came to church the next Sunday morning to find out what had made our girl so happy. He came several Sundays and then his life was wonderfully changed by Jesus. He went home one Sunday morning and said to his wife Hilda, 'I've given my heart and life to Jesus Christ'. Hilda had not the faintest understanding of what he was talking about. 'Len,' she said, 'no-one in our family has ever gone and got religion before. Why has it got to be you?'

But Len was changed. And Hilda noticed it. One evening, for instance, she was frying Len some dinner and as she went to put it onto the plate, one of the sausages fell on the floor. Hilda went rigid. She expected that Len would go through the roof or that he would project her through the roof. Len got up, took the plate from her hand, put the sausage back on it, said, 'Never mind, dear' and sat down to eat it. Hilda was amazed. She thought, 'This is not my Len'. However, she stuck it out for some months and then she said, 'Len, I don't know what it is that you've got, but whatever it is I want it too'. So she came to church and soon her life was changed.

Then three neighbours began coming, one after another, to find out what it was that had changed Len so wonderfully. And all this through a girl who forgot her words but when she spoke of Jesus 'she was so happy'.

Let your spirit speak as well as your words and let something of the joy of the Lord warm your heart as you speak and overflow to warm the hearts of others.

4. Don't press.

Your business is simply to share what you have, not to 'try to convert people' or put pressure on them. That sends them further away. Witness is not something *we* do for Jesus. It is something *He* does through us as we make the bridges in caring relationships and self-giving to others. I remember reading of a Christian on a bus who heard another Christian behind him witnessing to someone. While he told his own story the non-Christian responded with interest but when the Christian went on to press the gospel on his neighbour the interest went and was replaced by a defensive and finally a rejecting attitude.

Do not press people. Make your story clear and direct so that it makes sense but let it be an offer to the other, not a threat, and an offer to Jesus that He might use it by His Spirit.

When you have shared, by all means see if there is any more to be said or done by asking a simple question such as 'Have you ever felt you would like to know God personally?' If they respond positively then you can help them but if they answer negatively, do not press but later pray to God for them that He might continue His own work in their hearts.

Be sensitive and open to the person you are talking with and be sensitive and open to the Spirit of God. It may well be that your contact will be led to Jesus in a series of steps and over a long period of time, and God is asking you to be just the first of these steps. If you try to press people to two steps when as yet they are able only to take one, you will lose them. Your one step may be simply to raise the beginnings of an interest that by your care and prayer will continue to grow.

5. *Points to cover in your conversion testimony.*
The following are all elements it is a good idea to include when giving a testimony.
(a) What need or point of interest made you ready to hear the Good News of Jesus?
(b) How did you hear the Good News and how did you react?
(c) How did you come to commit your life to Jesus?
(d) How, precisely, did you do that?
(e) What difference has it made to your life?

Group exercises

1. Write out concisely your testimony (not necessarily your conversion experience) of what Jesus has done in your life, then share it with the group.

2. After each testimony is read let everyone say which

points they liked most about it and add one suggestion of something that might make it more crisp and challenging.

3. What do *you* think are the most important points about giving a good testimony?

4. Read Luke 24: 32–35, John 4: 27–42, John 9: 13–34, Acts 22: 1–22. What points of importance do you draw from the testimonies here?

5. Agree that during the next week everyone in the group will share their faith by speaking to someone of what Jesus has done for them.

If necessary, tell someone you know who is not a Christian, that within your house group you are discussing ways of telling others about Jesus Christ and that you have to tell your story to someone. Ask if they would mind listening and tell them!

Keep your written testimonies and take them out in a month's time to read again and rewrite in more direct and challenging form.

Chapter 7: Using Scripture to Share Your Faith

The New Testament is missionary literature, written in and for a missionary situation. The purpose of the Gospels may be summed up in John's words: 'These things are written that you might believe that Jesus is the Messiah, the Son of God, and that believing you might have life in His Name' (John 20: 31).

The Epistles are letters to young churches in the missionary situation. Some of our difficulties in understanding them today are because we neglect this context and read them from our own contemporary standpoint.

What the New Testament is

It is the most extraordinary fact that the early church, so full of life and witness, did not have a New Testament! It was only then being written. How, then, did people get to know about Jesus? It was through the Apostles.

In those days not many people could read and write. What they sought, when they wanted information, was 'a living witness' – one who was there and could say, 'This is what happened – I saw it. This is what was said – I heard it'. And this is what the twelve Apostles were. If you remember, when another Apostle was being chosen in place of Judas, one of the requirements was that he should be one who had been with Jesus 'from His baptism until the time of His resurrection' – a living witness (Acts 1: 21–22). Wherever the Apostles went in the ancient world, little groups of Christians would gather around them saying, 'Tell us more about Jesus. Tell us what you heard Him say. Tell us what you saw Him do'. And they would tell their stories. Sometimes particular stories would be told because of their relevance to the situation of the hearers at that time. But all of them witnessed to Jesus.

Whatever the meaning of the word 'Apostle' in later times, the Twelve had a calling and function which is unique and unrepeatable. They were the living witnesses to all that Jesus said and did.

However, when Peter was imprisoned in the time of Nero in 64 AD and looked certain to be killed, concern began in the Church. Suppose all the Twelve were to be put to death? Who then would bear the living witness? Who then would continue to tell what Jesus said and did?

There was one young man who had been around with Peter (and with Paul). He had heard Peter tell the stories of Jesus so many times that he knew them off by heart. He determined to write some of them down in a little book so that the 'living witness' of the Apostles might be preserved. We have this little book today. It is called the Gospel according to Mark.

After Mark, two enlarged and revised editions appeared. Luke and Matthew, and finally that tremendous drama which is John's Gospel. Here we have the first Apostles still bearing their witness: 'This is what Jesus said. This is what Jesus did'. But that is only half the story. When the Apostles preached they were not only relating the facts about Jesus as they knew them. They believed that Jesus was dynamically present by His Spirit to make those facts relevant and alive in the hearts of others. *And this is still true today*. When people read the Scripture with open heart, Jesus is present to change their lives.

How God uses Scripture

Stories of how God uses the Bible to change people's lives continue to pour out of the Bible Society, the Gideons and other organisations.[12]

There are a host of great stories. But my favourite story is of a Bible-seller in Sicily who set out one day with a sack of Bibles on his back intending to sell them in some villages on the other side of a forest. However, in the forest a bandit sprang out and held him up at pistol point. 'What have you got in that sack?' he asked.

'Only books,' said the Bible-seller.

'I don't want books,' replied the bandit. 'Gather up the sticks around. We'll light a fire and burn them'. The Bible-seller did as he was ordered and made a fire. He took the first Bible out of the sack and said, 'There's a marvellous story in this book. Before we burn it, let me read it to you'. So he read the story of the Good Samaritan.

'That's a good book,' said the bandit. 'I'll have that one'. And he took it and put it beside him.

The Bible-seller took another Bible and read the story of the Prodigal Son and again the bandit said, 'That's a good book. I'll have that one'.

After that it was Psalm 23, 1 Corinthians 13, the Sermon on the Mount and so on, until the bandit had all the Bibles beside him. Not one had been burnt.

'Now give me the sack,' said the bandit. I expect the Bible-seller felt like giving him the sack in a very different sense but he meekly handed the sack over. The bandit put all the Bibles in it and went on his way.

It was two years before the Bible-seller saw the bandit again. It was in the market square of a large town and the bandit was standing on a box and preaching about Jesus. When he saw the Bible-seller he ran and flung his arms around him saying, 'You will never know what difference your books made to my life'. The Bible-seller had no difficulty in knowing what difference the Bible had made to the ex-bandit's life – it was written all over him. In reading the Bible he had met with Jesus.

The Greek Orthodox Metropolitan Archbishop, Anthony Bloom, tells a moving story of how in his younger days he had begun to read Mark's Gospel, as much as anything to discover and to ridicule the Bible story. He says he had got no further than chapter three when he 'became aware of a presence' – the Living Word speaking to him through the written Word.

I remember during the Second World War I, together with some fellow servicemen, used to meet regularly for Bible study and worship at the Gospel Rooms in Valetta, Malta. We were of different denominations but no-one ever asked of what denomination we were.

One evening we were round a piano singing away when the door opened and there stood a stranger in naval uniform.

'Hello. Who are you?' we asked.

'I'm Eddie,' he said, 'I've just come out from Britain and I've just been converted'.

We sat him down and asked him to tell us his story.

He had been on board ship and had fallen ill. The ship's chaplain had come to see him. Eddie was not much interested in him – he had never been to Sunday school and had been to church only once and that was to get married.

The chaplain left behind a copy of the Gospel of Matthew and Eddie, having nothing else to do, began to read it. The story of Jesus was completely new to him and as he read it he became quite excited. This Jesus was such a surprising and wonderful man, not a religious fuddy-duddy at all. When he came to the threats against the life of Jesus he was quite sure God would never allow anyone to hurt Him – He was God's man.

When he came to the part where they crucified Jesus, Eddie was shocked and furious. He flung the Gospel away and told God very plainly what he thought of Him. 'He was your man,' said Eddie. 'Look at what He did for you. And look at what you let them do to Him. You're rotten!'

The chaplain came in a day or two later and Eddie was still angry. He told the Padre what he felt about the Gospel of Matthew, what he thought about God and what he thought about the Chaplain and his faith as well, all for good measure! Fortunately the Padre was a very patient man. He waited until Eddie had let off all his steam and then said, 'Just a moment, Eddie. You haven't read all the story yet'. He picked up the Gospel and showed Eddie how Jesus three times in that Gospel alone foretold His death and also His resurrection. He then took a New Testament from his pocket and showed Eddie how Jesus had said that He had come to die and that it would be for the sins of others.

When at last the truth penetrated to Eddie's mind, tough man though he was, the tears began to run down his cheeks and before long he was kneeling asking Jesus to change his heart and be Lord of his life.

I don't know if you can guess what strange thought went through my mind as Eddie told his story. It was 'I wish I hadn't read the Bible before'. To Eddie it was fresh, powerful and exciting. So often our trouble is that the story has become familiar, we think we know it all, we therefore do not expect to meet with Jesus afresh every time we read and our lives are not changed by meeting Him in His Word.

Why the Scriptures are written as they are

Some people are puzzled why God caused the Scriptures to be written in the way they are.

'Why not,' they say, 'have a first chapter headed "God" and under it everything the Bible says about God? Then a chapter headed "Jesus" and others headed "The Holy Spirit", "The Church", "The Christian Life" and so on?'

There are in fact books written just like that. This style is called systematic theology and is very useful if that is what you want. But the Bible is not a book of systematic theology. It is a book about God in the midst of everyday life.

In Oxford there are botanical gardens that display different kinds of grass. Each kind has a square to itself and is neatly labelled. I don't know who looks after it all and keeps it weeded but he has my admiration! This is systematic botany and very useful for those who are studying grasses. But grass does not grow like that in real life. Life is not in neat little compartments, all clearly labelled. It is higgledy-piggledy and all over the place. And that is exactly what the Bible is – life as it comes, with God in the middle of it all and the source and true meaning of it all.

Further, as we read the stories of the Bible we become aware of the stream of the Spirit of Jesus running through it all and drawing us into it so that our lives become part of the stream of the life of Jesus running through the circumstances and history of our own time.

I was fortunate in that when I was converted at the age of seventeen I went into a Christian Endeavour group. At the first meeting the leader explained the programme of the meeting to me. At one point, he told me that they had a 'prayer chain' and everyone prayed in turn. 'That's fine,' I said, 'but I can't pray in public'. The leader looked at me for a moment and then asked if I had anything I was grateful to God for. 'Oh yes,' I said, 'lots of things'. 'Right,' replied the leader 'just say "thank you" to God for one of them in one short sentence and then say "Amen" '. So I began to pray in public.

Later I was told that in sixteen weeks I would be the speaker at the meeting. I almost died! The subject was 'The salt of the earth' and the leader gave me all the Bible references to look up. Never have I worked so hard or so long in the preparation of a sermon as on that occasion and my talk lasted all of seven minutes! But I had begun to speak in public.

The leader also told me that we all read the same daily Scripture-reading notes. He gave me a copy and explained their use. He told me first to read the prescribed passage straight through. Then to read it through again, phrase by phrase asking 'What does it say and how does this speak to my life?' Following that I was to read through the passage a third time listening to the voice of God overall. Then – and not until then – was I to read the notes and see what God would say to me through the thoughts of someone else. Finally I was to come to prayer, beginning with what God had spoken to me about. So I began to read the Bible – not to debate it or simply to know what it said but to listen to the voice of God through it and to obey Him as His loved and loving child.

When you expose yourself to Scripture in this way, you can use it in witness. Its advantage is that you are not sharing a theory or an opinion but are sharing the Word of God. Because of the nature of the Bible there is an approach in Scripture for every circumstance and situation and always with that inner meaning which addresses itself to the inner being, the deepest needs and the very life-situation of man. The Bible is a meeting place with God. It is the preface to His presence, the footstool to His throne.

How to use a Gospel in witnessing

1. Know your Bible well through daily reading.
Sometimes in particular situations we have felt we know the mind and will of God. When we have asked ourselves, 'How do you know that this is God's will?' we have realised that in reading the Bible regularly over many years, accompanying God through so many life-situations and some like the present one, we have begun

to catch something of the set of His mind and the pattern of His ways. So we begin all unconsciously to let Him remould our minds into the likeness of His own.

2. *Learn those texts that speak deeply to you.*

Early in my Christian life I was encouraged to learn a text a day and during that day to let the mind brew on it and to 'suck it like a sweet'. In this way I learned a great number of texts and so many times since, in one situation or another, God has lit up one of those texts in my mind and made it live in my experience. Learn those texts or pieces of Scripture that speak deeply to you and they will be there, when you seek to share your witness, to help others.

3. *Carry two or three copies of your favourite Gospel.*

It is too expensive to give whole Bibles away and too much to carry several copies about with you. But you can carry and give away Gospels.

Begin by reading it through yourself in one sitting. Gospels were written to be read that way and you will then get the flow of the whole story. Thereafter read it through a paragraph a day and learn off by heart the texts that speak deeply to you. You are then ready to pray that God will give you His own opportunities to use a Gospel in sharing your faith. It is surprising then how many opportunities will come when it is apt and right to say, 'It is strange you should say that. Do you know there is a piece in the Bible that just speaks about that very thing' or 'answers that very question'.

Then is the time to produce a gospel, read the text or piece from it, underline it in pencil and give the gospel to the contact when you leave them. If you have truly been open and sensitive both to God and to the person, God can continue to use your witness and the Gospel to speak to the heart and mind of your contact. Don't speak about or underline too many texts or you will confuse your contact. Probably just one is best.

4. John's Gospel is best for texts.
John is full of great verses. Know by heart texts like 1:
12; 1: 18; 3: 16–17; 4: 14; 5: 24; 8: 12; 11: 25; 12: 24;
13: 34–35; 14: 1; 14: 6; 14: 27; 15: 5; 16: 33; 20: 20–29;
20: 31.

5. Luke's Gospel is best for stories.
Luke loves stories and parables. If you use these you
will not underline as you would a text but run your
pencil down the side of the margin to mark it.
  In Luke we have:
chapter 5: the story of Levi
chapter 7: the Pharisee and the sinful woman (and don't
miss the point that the Pharisee missed the blessing
because he regarded himself as a good man in need of
little forgiveness).
chapter 10: the good Samaritan
chapter 12: the rich fool
chapter 15: the lost sheep and the lost son
chapter 18: the Pharisee and the Tax Collector (a bad
figure in Jewish eyes because he worked for the forces
of occupation and many were dishonest).
chapter 18: the rich young ruler
chapter 19: Zaccheus
chapter 20: the vineyard
chapter 23: the cross and the penitent thief
chapter 24: the walk to Emmaus
What a wealth of great stories!

Use a modern translation

If you are a confirmed lover of the Authorised Version
with the beautiful language of 1611, by all means
continue to use it for yourself. I began my Christian life
with it and continually find that when I quote the Bible
it is this version which comes out. However, for those
who do not know the Bible a translation in modern and

plain English is best and we would recommend that you know and use a gospel in a modern version.

For intellectuals J B Philips' translation[13] is unbeatable but is rarely published in the form of cheap individual Gospels. For others the *Good News* translation is best.[14] It is published by the Bible Society and they will supply Gospels in quantity at cheap prices if they are to be given away. Creative Publishing[15] have some beautifully produced Gospels in either *Good News* or *New International Version* editions but at greater expense.

(1) *Finally* when you read your Bible be careful to concentrate deeply. Don't let your mind say 'Yes, I know that piece' and therefore slide over it. Listen and let the Spirit of Jesus speak to you afresh.

(2) Read the Scripture not to debate it or to choose from it the pieces you like. Read it to obey it.

(3) When using the Scripture in witnessing to another, let your heart and mind be wide open both to the other and to Jesus. Count on Him being livingly present, the Living Word speaking through the written and the spoken word.

Group exercises

1. Let everyone in the group share a Bible passage or text that has meant a great deal to them at some point in their life, and say why.

2. Each think of one person they would like to see become a Christian. Think of their circumstances, pick a piece of Scripture that might be especially helpful to them. Tell each other the kind of person you are thinking of, the Scripture you chose and what you might say (briefly) about it if you shared it with that person.

3. Each talk about what happened during the past week as they shared their testimony with someone.

4. Let each group member aim to share their faith with someone *this* week by using a piece of Scripture. If necessary tell a non-Christian friend you are in this group and ask if you may share a piece of Scripture with them as an exercise. Make an appointment to do so.

Chapter 8: The Use of Booklets in Faith-sharing

Sometimes, as well as using the Bible it is a good idea to make use of one of the many evangelistic booklets that have been published as an aid to faith-sharing. A booklet is a tool that God can and does use. Like all tools, before we use them we need to know about them and how best to use them before they can help us to do our work. A booklet is not a tract. A tract is a small leaflet to awaken someone's interest in God and can be given at random. A booklet is for use with someone who is interested in the gospel and can be used as a challenge to make them realise they have a commitment to make.

Often we have contact with people with whom we have shared our experience of Christ, answered their questions and talked with them over many weeks or perhaps over years. Maybe we feel they should be ready to face the challenge to commit their lives to Christ but we are not sure of the words to use to bring them to the point. If, like me, you do not have a logical mind, and find explaining things difficult or cannot remember the texts at the right time, a booklet can be a help. It is a tool that God can use but has no miracle powers of its own.

Booklets are, of course, only one of many ways of bringing people to see their need of Christ. They must not be used as an excuse for not knowing our Bibles thoroughly or getting to know people well enough to find out where they are spiritually. We must be sensitive too to know the kind of booklet which can be best used with the person with whom we are sharing.

Three booklets available

Journey Into Life by Norman Warren (Falcon Books)[16]

This could be given to an interested contact who is able to read and understand a clear presentation of the gospel with some illustrations. It brings the reader to a point of commitment, explains what to do then and after. It is available from Christian bookshops.

Coming Home (CPO)[17]

This is a very colourful booklet, useful for young people or anyone who reads more comics than books, and those who are not great readers. It could even be used to help someone who is unable to read. Once the pictures are explained a non-reader could probably understand it on their own. If they did not make a commitment to Christ that day, you could leave it with them and return some other time to talk about it.

The Four Spiritual Laws[18] or its revised version called *Knowing God Personally* (Campus Crusade for Christ)[19]. Material from *Four Spiritual Laws* is reproduced in Appendix 5 at the back of this book.

It is a small booklet with a very clear explanation of the gospel but with few pictures; it has a direct challenge to make a commitment to Christ. It is not suitable just to hand over to anyone, and leave them to read on their own. It is not attractive unless someone really wants to know about God, but is excellent when used as intended, sharing it with an enquirer.

When to use a booklet

If you are serious about wanting to share your faith with others and pray every day that God will give you an opportunity, always carry some booklets or tracts with you. It may be a chance meeting on a bus or train or at an airport when you meet someone whose heart God has prepared. Quite possibly you will be able to share only a little before you have to part, and you feel there are many more questions they would like answered. Pray in your heart for wisdom to give them the booklet that will be most helpful to them. If you know of a Christian near where they live or you can keep in touch write the address on the booklet itself. And pray regularly for your contact.

You may have a friend, member of your family, or someone you work with who has asked you many questions and you have been able to share your experience of Christ with them. God will show you, if you are sensitive to Him and them what kind of booklet would bring them nearer to an understanding of Him and what it means to make a commitment.

If you knock on doors in the area around your church building you could find someone really interested in the Christian faith. This is a wonderful opportunity, especially if they ask you in for a chat. Pray that God will make you sensitive to them so that you do not push them further than they are prepared to go on the first visit. Leave the right booklet and ask if you may call again.

May I emphasise the necessity of always following up such contacts personally – unless of course it is a fleeting one at an airport or some such place. When you have made a contact or given someone a booklet make an appointment to see them again soon and pray for them regularly. If it is someone you see regularly you can ask 'What did you think of the booklet? Was it a help?' We must be sensitive but we must not be embarrassed in doing the Lord's work.

Do know any booklets you carry thoroughly. Read them many times, prayerfully imagining questions or hesitations that might arise so that you are as prepared as possible for the Holy Spirit to use you.

In a previous chapter I mentioned Eric who found the Lord while attending a home Bible study group for new Christians. His wife, Rita, began to be interested and I visited her. After chatting we read through the *Four Spiritual Laws* booklet. When we came to the point of commitment I felt her hesitate so I simply left the booklet with her, promising to return a day or two later, and asking her to ponder over the booklet in the meantime. When I did go back I found a very joyful Rita who had made her commitment to the Lord.

Four Spiritual Laws is the booklet I have used much and often. (See Appendix 5.) One reason for this is that it begins on the right note: 'God loves you and has a wonderful plan for your life'. That is where the gospel really begins – 'God so loved. . . .' The booklet does not ignore sin (it is the second point) but most people are not helped by telling them they are sinners as a first point. Many feel unloved and inadequate anyway and can face the fact of sin only if they are assured of God's care and seeking for them. That is attractive.

The points of the *Four Spiritual Laws* are:
1. God loves you and has a wonderful plan for your life.
2. Man is sinful and separated from God. Thus he cannot know and experience God's love and plan for his life.
3. Jesus Christ is God's only provision for man's sin. Through Him you can know and experience God's love and plan for your life.
4. We must personally receive Jesus Christ as Saviour and Lord. Then we can know and experience God's love and plan for our lives.

Then comes the direct challenge. This is the page you will be reading out to the person beside you and they will give their own answer to the questions.

I am always amazed at how gently and naturally the crucial questions are asked and how regularly people answer honestly and face themselves with the challenge of commitment to Christ. The booklet then goes on to explain how people can turn from self and receive Christ as Lord.

Hints on using a booklet

1. You will use such a booklet only if you have found someone clearly interested in knowing God, you have listened to them lovingly and carefully and feel they are ready to face the challenge. Ask if you may read through the booklet with them.

2. Sit beside them, use only one booklet, holding it so that they can see the words, and if necessary putting your finger on the line as you read so that they follow it with you.

3. Stick exactly to the words of the booklet and don't be tempted to add your own comments or to preach a sermon. You will find as you read it slowly and meaningfully that the Holy Spirit will do His own speaking through the points and the Scriptures quoted.

4. You may be interrupted by a question. If it is a genuine question affecting the understanding of what you have just read, answer it and then continue. If it is a 'red herring' or not immediately relevant at that point say, 'Yes, that's a good question. But do you mind if I leave it until I have finished presenting this booklet?' If it is an honest question then do return to it afterwards and if it is one you cannot answer just say so and add 'If it is important to you, I will try to find the answer'. Never be afraid to say you don't know. And if you have promised to seek an answer keep your promise. A commentary or a relevant book will help, or failing that ask your minister.

5. Read the booklet slowly, clearly and meaningfully and perhaps stop from time to time to check that the person you are helping has followed and understood. Some points may be very new to them and will take a while

to see and accept. You may need to go back to a point. Occasionally as you read it becomes evident that the other person does not want you to continue or genuinely cannot understand. Then stop, try to find out where they are and in your heart ask God to guide you. It may be wise to leave things for the day, have a prayer with them and, if right, arrange to call again. With most you will leave the booklet for them to read but you may have a simpler tract or another booklet to leave with them.

6. When you arrive at the point of challenge in the booklet be very sensitive to the person beside you. Many times when I have shared the *Four Spiritual Laws* I have known the Holy Spirit move dynamically through the words spoken and the challenge is faced honestly and easily. However a commitment does not always follow right then.

Do not attempt to persuade someone to pray the prayer of commitment if they are not ready. If such a prayer is not from the heart it is mere repetition of words and God cannot honour it. Continue to listen and share but do not put any pressure on the person you are helping. The decision must be honestly theirs.

7. If the other genuinely wishes to pray the prayer of commitment, then first read the prayer through to them slowly. Check that this is what they want to say and if it is, give them the booklet and let them use the words there to make their commitment. Or they may prefer to repeat the words, phrase by phrase after you. Or again, they may wish to pray using their own words of repentance and commitment. How it is done is not so important as what is done. That must be understood and meant.

8. When a commitment has been made read the rest of the booklet with the person and make an appointment to return within two or three days. Leave the booklet with them and encourage them to look up all the references in their own Bible. If they haven't one get one for them quickly and explain how to use it. Pray with them before leaving.

9. Do keep any promises you have made and return within three days. If they have no or little background begin a short series of Bible reading and sharing sessions with them. Go with them to a Home Bible study and nurture group for new Christians so that they meet and share with others. If they have no other church connections and you feel they could cope with a Sunday service, then take them with you, sit with them and introduce them to other Christians.

The most important thing to remember is that a new Christian is a babe in Christ so must not be neglected. They need spiritual food and the love and care of the Christian family. It is your responsibility, as the one who led them to Jesus, to see that they are not left to die of spiritual starvation. If you cannot do this yourself (for instance, if you are just a visitor in that area) make sure it is done and done well by others. If the convert is of the opposite sex it might be wise to bring along someone of the same sex (if possible your husband or wife) when you visit and make the initial group a trio. If there is an age gap then, again, another person of similar age and same sex as the convert, may be helpful. When God has given you one of His divine appointments (and He will if you pray for them and are open) it must be followed up thoroughly.

A few years ago Lewis and I were doing a survey for a church in a northern city. One evening, Lewis went out door-knocking with another member of the church and I set off on my own. I went to a road Lewis and I had been prevented from visiting earlier in the afternoon due to rain.

At the very first house a man in his late thirties answered the door. I explained what I was doing and he asked me in. We sat in his front room and I began to ask the questions on the survey form. There were two questions about the neighbourhood and what he thought of it, two questions about life ('What is the most important thing in life for you?'), two questions about the churches and what he felt about them (the answers are sometimes unrepeatable!) and then two questions about God.

I had asked only a few questions when his wife put her head round the door wanting to see what was happening. She joined us and I began again and asked them both questions and listened as they talked. As they did so it became obvious that they were going through a time of trouble. Pauline, the wife, had been having what they thought were epileptic fits. It had upset the whole family and they did not know how to cope with it.

They answered all the questions and those about God were answered positively and warmly. I became aware of the presence of God and of His Spirit already in that situation. Their children went to the Sunday school at the church for which we were doing the survey and they themselves had met the minister.

Our survey is not in itself evangelistic but is to gain information about the feelings of people in the neighbourhood in order to plan for relevant evangelism. However, with such a positive response, we are always glad and ready to go on to share our faith on the spot.

I asked if they were willing to read through a booklet with me. I sat between them on the settee and began reading through the *Four Spiritual Laws*. We had not got far when Pauline turned to her husband, Harvey, and said, 'You're not really interested are you, dear?' This surprised me because I felt he was quite as interested as she was. However I gave Harvey a booklet to read through and continued with Pauline alone. She seemed able to forget her husband's presence as she faced the challenge of the gospel. Happily and naturally she committed her life to Jesus.

I then left her to continue reading the rest of the booklet while I read through Harvey's copy with him and he was just as earnest. God was wonderfully evident in that home that evening and before I left both were rejoicing in sins forgiven and the beginning of a new life together with Jesus as Lord. We had a time of tremendous blessing.

I returned to the home where we were staying, having been away three hours, to find Lewis, the minister and others praying for me! They had realised I must have been invited into a home and that something of importance was taking place. It was a joy to be able to hand over that pair to a live Christian fellowship in the city. Then we realised that if it had not rained in the afternoon, and I had called *then* at Harvey and Pauline's house, neither of them would have been in! God's ways and guidance are perfect.

It turned out that Pauline did not have epilepsy. She had a tumour on the brain and the family went through the trauma of watching her undergo major surgery. It was a test of their faith and of the sufficiency of Jesus in a time of trial. He did not fail them and, as always, worked all things for good and brought His meanings and purpose out of evil circumstances (Rom.8: 28 and Gen.50: 20 – two great texts to rely upon).

A note by Lewis:
At one time I would have been very much against any set and stereotyped approach such as the use of a booklet. However Molly has used them so much and has so often been blessed by God in doing so that I have had to say, 'Do not call unclean that which God uses'. I have come to realise that the Lord's theology is not always quite as sound as mine!

However, we ought to acknowledge one real disadvantage and that is that many of the booklets make it easy for the enquirer to make a 'private' decision which does not include a commitment to the People of God and to a life of commitment, service and obedience to Jesus.

A convert who has been brought to faith by the use of a booklet, therefore, should in due course be encouraged to make a public declaration of their faith, and should also be introduced quickly to a church house group and encouraged to weigh up the true cost of discipleship.

111

Group exercises

1. Obtain some copies of the three booklets mentioned in the chapter. In twos read the booklets one to the other in turn as though you were using them to present the gospel. (The one listening is to act the part of the 'model' interested non-Christian and not interrupt!)

2. Returning to the group, let each think out whether they would ever wish to use a booklet for witnessing and, if so, which one they would choose.

3. Each share what happened during the past week as you shared the faith with someone by using a piece of Scripture.

4. Each share your faith with someone this week by using a booklet (or, alternatively, if you have the training, by the Teach and Reach (Evangelism Explosion) method: see Ch 12). If necessary ask a friend and set up an appointment.

Chapter 9: The Spirit in Which We Share

From a heart filled with Jesus

One Monday morning our doorbell rang. I went and there stood a man who said in a strong Cockney accent 'Are you the man who sent the letters?' (We had been sending monthly letters to four thousand homes in the neighbourhood.) I was not sure, if I owned up, whether he would thank me for them or hit me on the nose, but I said I was. 'I'm in terrible trouble,' he said. I asked him in and we sat down. 'I daren't go to work and I daren't go home,' he admitted. My mind replied 'Well by the sound of it you are going to be a long time in that chair,' but my lips said, 'Tell me about it'.

He said, 'I've got gambling fever in my blood. I just can't stop gambling. I keep getting into trouble and now I'm fifty pounds in debt to the works bookmaker. I can't pay it and he says he won't wait any longer for his money. I just dare not go to work today. Even worse, last time I was in trouble my wife told me she'd leave me if I gambled once again so I just daren't go home'.

We talked for a short time and then I said, 'Do you believe in God?'

'Oh, yes,' he replied, 'I do'.

'Right,' I said, 'let's begin there. Let's pray to Him and ask Him to give you His strength and to guide you'. We knelt down and I prayed asking God to give him victory over his compulsion to gamble and to help him to a new life in Jesus. When we got up he looked at me a bit sheepishly and gave me an attaché case which he had brought with him. I opened it. It was crammed with books supposed to help the gambler. They must have cost quite a lot.

I looked at them and thought, 'They haven't been of much use to him and they won't be of much use to me either!'

So the two of us went out to our kitchen and dropped the books one by one onto the boiler as a kind of burnt offering to God! We returned and talked some more. 'If you are serious about giving up gambling and finding God,' I said, 'you will be greatly helped by having a loving, praying group of people around you giving you strength and support. Had you thought of coming to church?' 'No,' he replied, 'I couldn't come to church'. I asked why not and I suppose he answered with the first thing that came into his head, 'I've got no clothes to come in' (quite untrue for he was wearing some at the time!) 'Come just as you are,' I said – which is, after all the gospel invitation.

He left and I phoned the works bookmaker and arranged for the man to pay off his debt bit by bit and then went to see his wife. She had no intention of leaving him, good woman. She just wanted him kept straight.

The next Sunday morning I entered the pulpit and saw this man, Harold, sitting there in the back pew, looking rather nervous and apprehensive. I just said in my heart 'Father, please touch that man and bless him. Give him your peace and let him know that you love him.'

As we sang the opening hymn the door at the back opened and a young man slipped into the back pew right beside Harold. He was a boy who had been trained to share his faith with others and I thanked God for the first miracle. Fancy there being room in the back pew of a church after the service had begun! After the service I went down the aisle, keeping one eye on the back pew.

I saw our young man shake hands with Harold and begin talking with him.

That evening Harold was there again but this time up in the gallery with his wife and two children. In that church the evening service was a thing of power and blessing. The church was always packed with loving, praying people. Harold went away that night knowing that he had found something rich and beautiful. He was not sure what it was but God was in it. He went home and wrote me a nine-page letter. I got it on the Tuesday morning. It was in his own cockney language entirely and as I read it I thought to myself, 'I'm not sure how many people could understand this'. It ended by saying 'Cor blimey, my heart is singing "Open up your heart and let the sunshine in!" ' I know that that hymn is not yet in our hymnbooks but I reckoned that the angels of God were rejoicing about it!

A week or two later Harold came to me and said, 'I want to join as a member of this church and so does my wife'. I said, 'Praise the Lord! You know the condition, don't you, that you have committed your whole lives in trust and obedience to Jesus Christ. Have you done that?' 'Yes,' he answered, 'we have, after the service last Sunday evening'. He and his wife attended membership classes, were baptised and received into membership.

The very next Thursday I came to conduct the Bible study and prayer meeting. He sat right by the door and as I came in he pressed a piece of paper into my hand. I opened it and it read, 'When it comes to the prayer time please ask me *by name* to pray. Otherwise I shan't have the courage'. I conducted the Bible study and then said, 'Harold will now lead us in prayer' and I sat down. He got up and began to pray, falteringly and in his own words but within a few sentences that prayer just took wings and there was no-one in the room that night who did not feel deeply and profoundly moved. What Harold poured out was this: never in his wildest dreams had he imagined that God would have any time for him. God would have time for good people. God might have time for church people. But he was neither a good person nor a church person. He felt if God ever noticed him at all then He could only condemn him out of hand. But now, in the midst of his waywardness, God had burst in, had opened the heavens and would not stop pouring upon him love and mercy and grace and goodness and blessing. He could not get over it and as he stood and prayed all the wonder, the praise and the gratitude of a heart filled with God's grace poured out in that prayer.

The next day I was in the main road as he was coming from his work at an aircraft factory. He hurried over to me and said, 'I've just been telling the men at work about Jesus. They said I was different and asked me why'. Harold did not have to be told that now he was a Christian it was his duty to witness to Jesus. You could not have stopped him if you had tried! The joy and wonder of it came flowing out at the simplest opportunity in his life and in his words. It was as natural as it was genuine.

The spirit in which we witness is to be precisely that – the natural and genuine overflow of a heart filled with Jesus, His grace, mercy and His love, in such measure that it cannot be kept in. When witness becomes a thing we have to do as a duty it is already dead. The pity of it is that in so many churches the new convert comes in blazingly keen and is not taught how to combine his readiness to share with sensitivity and within a year or two is dulled down in both. That such a thing should be is a grave indictment of a church and of church members. Perhaps our first and greatest need today is to get down on our knees and, like little children, allow His love to be shed abroad in our hearts by the Holy Spirit whom He has given to us.

Christian witness contrasted with proselytism

I would now like to contrast Christian witness sharply with proselytism, this being an aggressive attempt to 'convert' someone at all costs – in other words witness from the wrong spirit and the wrong motive.

1. Proselytism is self-seeking.

Some time ago I was asked to be moderator at a small village church that had no minister. It was a pleasant duty and I enjoyed it. All went well until we came to their annual general meeting, which I chaired. The secretary gave us a good report on the year. Then the treasurer got up and had to report that the cause was £200 the poorer than last year. Obviously he felt he might be blamed for this for he began to harangue the small band of people before him.

He wagged his finger and said, 'It's your fault our funds are down. During the coming year I want you to go out into the village and bring the people in. Bring in your friends, bring in your neighbours and fill up the empty pews so that when I stand here next year I shall not have to report that the funds are down.'

I was amazed! I had heard of a good number of motives for witness before but not that we might be in funds! But although we might chuckle at the treasurer (who I am sure did not mean things that way) we must admit it is difficult to escape the temptation of the human mind that wants to see success. When other Christians ask us how our church is doing we want to reply, 'Just great'. We want to belong to a successful church and to think we are effective witnesses and are 'doing very well'.

But when we and our ambition become the centre of our gaze and not Jesus and His heart alone, then pride rises up. The church becomes *our* church, the guardian of *our* traditions and witness becomes pew-filling, building for *our own* preservation or success. *This is proselytism and it is a constant temptation.*

Years ago there was a slogan in vogue 'Evangelise or perish'. It always worried me. If we are going to evangelise merely for the sake of not perishing then it would be better to perish. If we are one with Jesus we witness because we cannot help it. His love leaves us no choice and will insist on overflowing naturally and genuinely into every part of life. That is Christian witness.

2. Proselytism seeks to patronise.

When Jesus sent out the seventy-two in twos He said He was sending them out as 'lambs among wolves' (Luke 10: 1–6). That, like so much that Jesus said, turns all our ways upside down and from the earliest days to the present we have always sought to turn them back again. We want to go out as wolves among lambs! We want to go out as the strong ones, telling people what they ought to hear and what they ought to do. We want to feel superior to those who do not know Jesus. We want to play the Lady Bountiful who could go from her nice mansion to visit the slums to give her smiles and help and advice and then go safely home again to her mansion.

Early in this century the Church had position, status and pride. Churchgoers were looked up to because they went to church and lived good lives. Now we are looked upon as odd, as those who are a bit queer in the head. All our props have been taken from us. Some people are sad about that and would like to recapture the Church's strength in this world. I am glad the props have gone and we are left with the living Christ and His Spirit and with Him only. We go out as lambs among wolves but we do not go alone. For that reason I like D T Niles' definition of evangelism as 'one beggar telling another beggar where he may get bread'. One beggar cannot be superior to another beggar. They stand on the same level. They are the same in everything except that one has found bread (the bread of life) and can tell another where to find it. Our safety and confidence should not be in any feeling of superiority but in Jesus alone. The human temptation is always to look for props or some superiority. That is why churches go a mile down the road to evangelise the working-class estate rather than witness to their better off neighbours. That is why children's work is so popular and witnessing to our friends and neighbours is not. We want to be wolves among lambs.

Proselytism seeks to patronise. But in Christian witness there is no possibility of patronising because we live moment by moment by the grace and redeeming mercy of God alone and ever will do.

3. Proselytism makes us want to witness on our own terms. Some time ago we were working with a church which had had a youth evangelistic team leading a campaign there two weeks before. One of the leaders of the church was not pleased about it and said to us privately, 'They have brought in all the riff-raff of the town. It will take us at least a year to get rid of them'. We could not believe he was serious, but he was. He would never have approved of Jesus!

E H Robertson tells a story about how he went to take a harvest festival service in a village. It was the tradition there that everyone turned out for the harvest festival and the place was packed. Normally they had only the faithful eight or nine. Robertson conducted the service and afterwards went to one of the old stalwarts and said, 'Wasn't it great to see the church full?'

'Maybe,' said the old faithful, 'but I like it best when it's just us'.

Proselytism makes us want to pick those we witness to, those who are like us, those who will be useful to us, those who will be 'respectable' and those who will not alter the status-quo. Christian witness cannot work like that. It witnesses to anyone just as God gives the opportunity and it remains sensitive to the person and to God.

Molly has a natural gift for talking to people and for door-to-door visiting. I have not. I have had to learn by hard experience. When I first began to do door-to-door work and was faced with someone on the doorstep I knew clearly what *I* wanted for the person before me and spoke with enthusiasm. But I soon discovered that my wants for the other were being projected onto the situation as a pressure which made my contact withdraw. Instead of truly meeting them and building the bridge of a personal relationship and letting the Holy Spirit do the rest, my own desires were putting up barriers both between myself and the other person, and between myself and the spirit. I have had to learn to relax, to have no preconceived notions or desires for this short meeting except to be open to the contact and to Jesus. I have had to learn that God may intend my visit simply to be the first step in many steps that will lead the other to Christ and to try to push him to take two steps when he can take only one is to cause him to step back, not forward.

Once this is learned it gives a wonderful freedom in meeting and relating to people – and in relating to people in daily life as they are and as they come. Christian witness is often unconscious and when it is conscious it is natural, loving and genuine – the love of Jesus overflowing.

4. Proselytism forces converts to conform.
A new convert, naturally, will tend to adopt the forms and expressions of Christianity he finds in his first fellowship. This is not necessarily bad but it does need to be pointed out; and we need to be clear that Christianity is not the same thing as the forms in which we clothe it. However, we are here speaking of something further – of a tendency in a local congregation (more marked in rigid, immature or uncertain fellowships) to mould purposefully the ways of the new convert to cause no stir or challenge to themselves.

120

We were in Watford in the early 'fifties, in the days of the 'Teddy-boy' gangs. There were a number of them around our church and we made friends of some of them. They were just kids with little maturity, purpose or feeling of significance and it was better to throw a stone through a window and be chased and sworn at than not to be noticed or counted at all. One gang leader began to bring his gang to church every Sunday. We had refreshments in the hall afterwards with a time for chatting and getting to know one another. One evening he came and took out his great sheath-knife and handed it to me to look at. In Teddy-boy cirlces this was an act of friendship! I said, 'Very nice' or something else equally untrue and he returned it to its sheath (for which I was most grateful). Then he said to me, 'Do your people mind that I wear Teddy-boy clothes?' I said, 'I'm sure they don't', and he replied, 'Then why do they keep saying to me, "We don't mind what clothes you wear"?' A very perceptive observation!

Ours was a wonderful working-class congregation of loving people but despite themselves they could not help looking at him out of the corner of their eye and thinking, 'He's not become a Christian yet or he wouldn't wear Teddy-boy clothes'. In the end he and his gang wandered off and did not return. This was a huge shame as Molly and I had prayed that this Teddy-boy would be gloriously converted by the grace of the Lord Jesus and that he would continue to wear his Teddy-boy clothes and witness to other Teddy-boys in the neighbourhood as only he could.

Proselytism wants to make everyone alike, a conforming, non-challenging club. But Christian witness aims to allow the Holy Spirit to set everyone free to be their own true selves in Christ; one with every other and different from every other. Wherever God puts down His hand there is tremendous variety within unity. Our witness must reflect and rejoice in that.

5. *The proselytiser wants instant results*.

It is rarely that we work with a church without being told 'You will find it very hard round here'. In fact it is usually not so. People are just people. They do not want to be pushed or have religion thrust down their throats but they rarely object to meeting someone friendly and caring who will share, if opportunity offers, something of his own heart and experience. Witness, without caring, is patently ineffective. If you asked people who live close to our church buildings what the churches are known for, they would answer 'religion' or 'meetings'. Perhaps our witness will begin to make sense when our churches are known for their unfailing love.

One of the books that moved me most profoundly when I first read it is *No Language But a Cry* by Richard D'Ambrosio. It is the true story of a married couple, both alcoholics, and the baby born to them whom they named Laura. They were so far gone in alcohol that they could not look after themselves properly much less this little baby. Laura was neglected and treated badly.

They lived in an area where no-one took very much notice of such things, but one day the screams of the little child were so bad that the neighbours called the police. The police went in to find the wretched couple – totally befuddled by alcohol – frying Laura in a frying pan over the fire. Laura was taken to hospital and by a miracle she lived, but her mind was badly damaged. They discharged her saying, 'We have done all we can for her burned and battered body. That is now fit but we can do nothing for her mind'.

She was labelled schizophrenic, although had she been discharged today the label would not have been schizophrenic but autistic. Laura's experience had been so traumatic that her subconscious had decided that the outside world was too horrific and agonising to face. A shutter had come down in her mind that cut off the outside world from her feelings or any kind of relationship. She was sent to a children's home and each day she was led into the playroom and immediately crouched against one wall. Around her lots of children were playing merrily with toys and tumbling over each other but little Laura sat there huddled up into a ball and living totally within herself.

Richard D'Ambrosio was the psychiatrist for that home and took up Laura as one of his patients when she was twelve years old. She was brought to his office two afternoons a week and he talked to her. He talked about anything and everything he could think of that might possibly interest Laura and draw her out of herself. After a year he was finding it difficult to find anything else to talk about and Laura had shown no response whatever. He did not even know whether she knew he was there. In sheer desperation in the second year he bought a large doll's house construction kit and every time Laura came in he would pull out the boxes, take out pieces and build another part of the doll's house – talking and working at the same time in front of Laura.

At the end of the second year he had completed the doll's house and Laura still had not shown any kind of response. Nevertheless he felt in his bones that she was beginning to be interested. So he bought the kits to build the doll's house furniture and again each time Laura came to him he would work away, talking about everything and explaining everything he did. He had one day finished the furniture for the kitchen and had set in a table and four chairs. But one chair he had put in carelessly and a little hand suddenly came past his hand and put the chair in place! Laura did not move again but now he knew she was with him and following everything he did.

A little later he felt the time was ripe to try a daring experiment. He bought a father doll, a mother doll and a baby doll and played out scenes with them in the doll's house as though they were the real people living there. One day he made the father and mother doll have a blazing row and begin to beat the baby. This was Laura's

123

own story being played back to her. She went deathly white and suddenly screamed 'No! No! No!' – the first words anyone had ever heard her say although she was obviously able to speak and used words in her own mind.

Richard D'Ambrosio tells us that from that point he began to see Laura's life open up to him as shyly and gradually as a flower opening to the sun. After another year he was talking to Laura and she was talking back to him. When she was eighteen, after six years' therapy with D'Ambrosio, Laura was discharged from his care as a perfectly normal and happy girl able to get a job as a children's nurse.

That book moved me deeply for its own sake but when I put it down at the end I prayed, 'Lord Jesus, please teach me how to love people. And please teach us as churches how to love people with your love'. Too often we hold a ten-day 'campaign' and for those ten days we pray for people, care for people and visit people. The butcher, the baker and the candlestick maker are all lost souls for whom Jesus died and we feel His compassion for them. But when the ten days are over everything returns to where it was. We no longer visit the people. We no longer pray for them. They are just the butcher, the baker and the candlestick maker again. We write up the campaign glowingly in the magazine and we praise the Lord that 'five people were converted'. For the rest of the community we merely grumble, 'They are hard around here. They don't wish to see what we have to show them or to hear what we have to tell them'. And then I think of Richard D'Ambrosio and Laura who did not see and did not hear, and how he went on pouring out loving care on that little child, year in and year out, whether she responded or not, until at last her eyes began to be opened and her ears unstopped.

God has called us into our local church fellowships that we might learn how to love with His love, first to love one another and then to let love overflow to the neighbourhood. Let love and light and life pour out like a fountain, whether people respond or not, year in and year out unceasingly until eyes that are blind begin to see Jesus and ears that are stopped begin to hear His voice.

So many of our 'campaigns' are no more than wild raids and some are merely proselytism. Christian witness is the love of Jesus beating in the heart of His Body and pouring out unceasingly and without bounds to all around. The spirit in which we witness is the same Spirit that we saw in Him.

Group exercises

1. Get someone with a good reading voice to read out 1 Corinthians 13 (including the first phrase in chapter 14 which belongs to this passage). Each rewrite the chapter in terms of your own life situation. For instance, a teacher might write 'If I can speak on my subject with skill and accuracy but do not care at all about those I teach, I fail as a channel of the love of Jesus . . .' After fifteen minutes let each share in turn what they have written. Spend a time of prayer together.

2. Let each group member talk about what happened during the past week as they have shared their faith with someone using a booklet (or other pattern of presentation).

Part III:

The Church in Witness –
Methods and Motivation

Chapter 10: The Church and its witness

The House of God is His people

It is not often that I commend the Living Bible because it is a paraphrase of Scripture. A paraphrase can be very helpful and if that is what you want the Living Bible will serve you well but it is not a translation. But I would commend its interpretation of 1 Corinthians 3: 16: 'You together,' says Paul, 'are the House of God and the Spirit of God dwells among you in His House'. The Living Bible brings Paul's sense out well because it makes it clear that Paul is not addressing the individual but the church at Corinth.

In the Old Testament we read about the Israelites in the desert with the tabernacle (the symbol of the presence of God among His people) pitched in the middle of the camp. It is significant that John says of Jesus, 'The Word was made flesh and tabernacled among us'. Later the symbol of God's presence was the temple and this is often referred to as the House of God (of Psalms like 84, 122 or 135). There are a lot of Christians who still think in Old Testament terms and refer to a church building as the House of God. But the New Testament will have none of this. Jesus assured the Samaritan woman that where you worshipped was a matter of indifference to God and when Jesus died the veil of the temple was rent in two from the top to the bottom. No longer would God be confined to a temple made by human hands.

In the New Testament the House of God is His people.

Jesus lives in the living fellowship of His people and the life they share together is His risen life. He builds them up together as living stones to be the temple in which He dwells.[21] If all the church buildings fell down tomorrow the Church of Jesus would still be there – and perhaps more lively than before – because the house in which Jesus lives is His people. Peter also calls the church a priesthood and the work of the priesthood is to represent man to God in prayer and to represent God to man in witness.

However, one of the most seminal pictures of the Church in the New Testament is as the Body of Christ and to this we now turn.

The Body of Christ

There are many people who have said, 'I wish I had been with Jesus when He was here upon earth. I wish I had seen the expression on His face when He said these words or those. I wish I had been able to touch Him. I wish I had been with Him in the body'. The New Testament makes it clear that there is no way of having true fellowship with Jesus except in the Body – and that Body today is the living fellowship of His people.[28] That is the nitty-gritty of the living of the Christian life. The church (the living fellowship of believers) is the Body of Christ. It is there that Jesus lives and it is through His Body that He is to be manifest to the world.

The Church on Monday

Everyone knows where the church is at eleven o'clock on Sunday morning. It is there in the church building, gathered together like the fingers of the praying hands to praise God, to pray to Him and to receive His Word. But where is the church at eleven o'clock on a Monday morning? It is as though Jesus has spread out His fingers and placed them on a map of the area. There are the members of the Body of Jesus touching every part of everyday life.

Let us stress that you are as much in the church on Monday morning at the sink or in the office or factory or workshop as you are in the church building on Sunday morning. You are always in the church for you *are* the church. The life of the local church is not just in its meetings on church premises. Its life is the life of its members out there in the world every moment that they live and in every situation.

Further, we need to stress that for the Christian 'secular' work *is* Christian service. If God has not called you to be elsewhere, He has called you to be where you are, rendering every part of your life (your home, your work, your relationships and your leisure) to Him that by His spirit it may burn with His glory and serve Him as your true worship (Rom 12: 1–2). And we are there to serve Jesus not as isolated individuals but as members of the Body – joined to other members, sharing the one life of Jesus, sharing with one another, open to one another and supporting one another – the Church present in the world as yeast is in the batch of baking.

People say that there is a gap between the Church and the world. But how can there be when day after day we are out there in the world? The truth is that the gap is in us. Instead of being the people of God present in the world we have become a dual people. Christianity is for Sundays and for our private lives, not for everyday living. Consequently we have reversed the order of things that Jesus gave us. We are not in the world; mentally we keep ourselves separated (like the Pharisees) in case we get contaminated. But we are too often *of* the world. We are not those whose values, attitudes and spirit, whose love and joyful generosity (the manifestations of the presence of Jesus) make us extraordinary in the living of everyday life.

We are called to be members of the Body in which Jesus lives and through which He expresses Himself and does His work. We are to be the touch-points at which other people become aware of His presence. Let me explain what I mean by a touch-point. I was demobbed from the Royal Air Force in 1947. If anyone had come to me at that time and had said, 'You are a young and single man. We have a lovely young lady here called Molly Hill who would be a wonderful wife for you. We think you ought to begin courting her,' I would have refused outright. I would have said, 'I don't know Molly Hill and I am not the least bit interested in getting to know her'. But I then joined a witness group (a National Young Life Campaign Group) and one winter evening I stomped through thick snow to get to our meeting place. The meeting was about to start when the door opened and in came a girl who had just driven seven difficult miles in a butcher's van to get there. I was impressed. I said to the fellow beside me, 'Who is that girl?' and he replied 'Molly Hill'. I was immediately interested in Molly Hill! I wanted to know her more and the more I got to know her the more I liked her. Finally I asked her to be my wife and today she is my chosen beloved, Molly Misselbrook. Sometimes we are surprised or disappointed when we speak about Jesus to others and they are not interested. But why should they be? What is needed is a touch-point from God that makes them say to themselves, 'There is something good or attractive here' so that they begin to be interested and want to know more.

And that is exactly what our lives are to be, touch-points for Jesus in the daily life of the world. That is to be the Church of Jesus present in the world.

Someone has said you can lead a horse to water but you can't make it drink, to which the retort has been made, 'No but if you put salt in his oats you can make him very thirsty.' We are to be as salt, making people thirsty for God. This is our basic and continuous witness.

What flows out?

Ray Stedman[23] tells a story of a visit he made to an oil refinery in California. On a guided tour he was shown the works with one great machine after another, every one of them noisy and busy. He was impressed. At the end of the tour the guide asked the party if they had any questions and Ray Stedman asked, 'How many thousands of gallons of oil are you sending out from this station every day?' The guide looked abashed and replied, 'Well, the station once did well and we hope it will do so again. But at the moment we produce only just enough oil to keep it going'.

How many churches are there like that? A guided tour will take you to the creche, then on to the beginners' department, the juniors, seniors, Bible class and to all the many meeetings of the church. All of it is so busy and so impressive until you ask 'How much of the love and goodness of Jesus is flowing out every day from this church to the neighbourhood round about?' Only too often the true answer would be 'Very little. We just about produce enough life to keep the organisation busy and running and no more'.

How a way of evangelism is born

We were in the Midlands at a meeting when we met a man of seventy-two who had led twelve people to the Lord through the Evangelism Explosion method (see Ch.12). One of the converts, a man of twenty-eight, was also there and told us his story.

The older man had knocked on his door on a cold, wet, winter night and introduced himself and two others as visitors from the church. The younger man was annoyed at being brought from the warm room and the television and said aggressively, 'How old are you?'

'Seventy-two,' replied the visitor.

'Then you ought to be at home with your feet up,' said the young man, 'what do you want to come worrying people for on a night like this?' The older man replied, 'I love Jesus and I love you and I would like to introduce you to each other'. 'And he really meant it,' said the young man telling the story. 'I looked at him for a moment and then I asked him in and he led me to Jesus that night'. 'I love Jesus and I love you.' These are the words that, if they are true, make our lives a bridge between Jesus and those who do not know Him.

Do we really love Jesus? Not just respect Him or even reverence Him. Do we love Him? Above all else? Do we love people? Those who live around us. Those we work with. Do we love them and know the compasssion of Jesus for them? Have they any reason to feel that we love them? Where the leaders of a church really know a love for the Lord and a love for the people of the town or the neighbourhood around them, a way of church evangelism will be born. Where there is the pain of loving Jesus and loving people who do not know Him and the pain is felt in prayer and sharing and in an opening of themselves to the Holy Spirit a way will come to birth which is the right way for this place and this time.

A bridge, if it is to carry traffic, has to be firmly founded on both sides. So we need to be firmly founded in and totally committed to Jesus and firmly founded and compassionately immersed in our town or neighbourhood. Then God will give us those plans and visions which are of His Spirit and which are truly relevant to our community.

Be known

It is always difficult for church people to believe that non-church people do not even notice church buildings and still less do they know what churches do or stand for. Molly was in hospital at one time and found herself in a bed beside a lady who lived in the next street to that of our church building. Molly was surprised to find she had no idea where it was although it was a lively church and she must have walked past the building most days of the week.

At one time we were doing a survey for a Baptist church and I knocked on the doors of three houses about two hundred yards up the road from the church building. Among my questions I asked, 'Can you tell me where the nearest Baptist church is?' One said they had no idea. The second said, 'There is a church down the road – is that a Baptist?' Only the third said she knew where it was although all three could see the building from their doorsteps.

When I got back to the office I told this story to my secretary who showed a distinct disinclination to believe it! So I said to her, 'You come up from the station to the office every morning and return every evening. Tell me what shop is on the corner opposite the bank.' She could not do so and I said to her, 'Just as you pass that shop every day and don't notice it, because it is irrelevant to you, so people pass church buildings without seeing them'. One of our first needs is simply to be known as loving and caring agents of Jesus.

So the need arises to build a bridge between ourselves and those around us. Here are three bridge-building methods we can use:

1. The use of Literature

(a) Letters. If you have someone who can write a letter that is simple, warm and loving then use them to write a letter once a month to everyone in the neighbourhood. It needs to be printed or reproduced to look like typing on the church's notepaper (perhaps you had better get some more attractive church notepaper first!) and put into envelopes personally addressed. The addresses you get from the electoral roll and/or a local directory

135

and if you can, get a member in each road to check the lists and bring them up-to-date. The letters are then delivered by church members. It is important to do as large an area as possible but no more than you can be certain of continuing to cope with over the months. There is nothing worse than starting well and then tailing off as volunteers fall away. A break should perhaps come in July and August. Otherwise let the letters be a regular touch in people's lives for about a year. This will bring an interest from many people who are ready to respond actively to the message of Jesus (one in 240 is the average) and is a good preparation for any other kind of evangelistic outreach following.

The content of the letters should be simple. There should be no attempt to put over heavy doctrine but just a pouring out of the love of Jesus to ordinary people and His longing that they should bring to Him their sins, their sorrows and their lives. The style of the letters should also be simple. No stiff, stylised or ecclesiastical English but a personal, warm and direct style and with some humour.

The letters should be short. Two hundred words a time is sufficient – people will not read long letters from a church. They should be signed by the minister although he may not be the one who writes them. The person with the best 'warm print newspaper style' is the one for that although it may be the minister who drafts the content.

It could be good to begin your regular letters by sending a genuine, loving Christmas card (preferably at Christmas!) not trying to get people to come to the Christmas services but giving a truly loving and truly Christian greeting.

(b) A neighbourhood newssheet. We have been surprised how often non-church people have expressed appreciation that a local church sends them their magazine regularly. It has made some real contact. We have been surprised because most church magazines are not

at all slanted toward non-church people. They usually tell you who gave the flowers last Sunday and who is speaking at the Women's Pleasant Hour next Wednesday and these are not items to cause undue excitement in the heart of the unbeliever.

It is much better if the church has a paper (like a small newspaper of just four pages) or a newssheet (A4 folded to make four pages) especially orientated toward the non-churchgoer, and delivered free to the whole neighbourhood. It should deal with topics of interest and concern in the neighbourhood – letting events of the neighbourhood form the contents but letting Jesus give the comments and the answers. Things of topical and general interest are written up simply and shortly from a Christian point of view and there may be a 'message from the minister' (not more than two hundred words) at the end of each edition. Some newsletters of this kind, attractively produced and presented, are doing excellent service today.

(c) *Seasonal tracts and leaflets.* General material is usually not as good as that which is personal and local but there is a wealth of good general material on the market. The Bible Society produce beautiful leaflets for special times like Christmas, Easter and harvest and the Christian Publicity Organisation produce excellent general material for all times of the year. It is worth being on the mailing list of both organisations (see Notes 14 and 17 at the end of this book). The material can be overprinted with a local address or short message or can be rubber-stamped with the name and address of a church or a street representative.

Wherever there is a general distribution of material to the neighbourhood, of whatever kind, the members must be prepared to use it as a talking point and to share their faith personally when it is natural and right to do so. Literature does not, on its own, produce more than a warm opportunity for further witness either by members personally or through some church outreach method.

2. The prospect list

A prospect list is useful if your resources are limited and your neighbourhood is large. It cuts down the number of homes you deliver literature to but at the same time does decrease the value of it as a general talking point in the area. A prospect list is drawn up during a preliminary visitation of the area. A team (perhaps students on vacation) call door-to-door. They already have names and addresses from the electoral roll and check these by greeting each householder by the name on the list. Then they say, 'We are doing a survey of this area. Could you tell me, please, if you attend any church or any place of worship?' If the people say they do not, then the 'No' box is ticked beside their name. This usually goes for about half the population. If people say they have had some contact with a church the interviewer will write down the church's name.

Sometimes people answer vaguely 'I'm Church of England' or something else. In which case the interviewer says 'That's fine. Do you actually go there on Sundays to worship?' Then the procedure is as before.

The lists are then taken and rewritten into lists under the heading of each church, giving names and addresses of people who say they go there. The lists are then sent to the ministers of those churches. Who is more surprised – the minister to see the list of people who say they are connected with his church or the people if he actually calls on them, I don't know! But these people are thereafter left to the care and witness of the church they claim to attend. Often the connection is slight but it does give a good opportunity for the church they name to build on the connection. It is also a good piece of co-operation with other churches in the area, creating goodwill and preventing any suspicion of 'sheep stealing'.

However, all those who admit to not attending any church are your prospect list. To them a suitable team will regularly deliver letters, newsletters or leaflets and will, after the first three or four deliveries, knock and hand in the literature personally. They need to be simply trained and prepared so that if people want to talk or ask them whey they come, they can share their faith plainly, lovingly and genuinely.

In drawing up the prospect list one or two (usually very few) hostile people are discovered. With most of these it is wiser not to include their names on the list but, if God lays them upon your heart, get a prayer triplet praying for them in that street.

3. The Watch and Pray Group

Watch and Pray Groups are groups of Christians who live in the same street or in three or four adjacent streets. They meet once every other week for Bible study and sharing but their main concern is a pastoral one for the street, streets or sub-area in which they live. The group watches out for newcomers in those streets and goes to welcome them and give news (verbally and duplicated on church notepaper) of local facilities – shops, doctors, churches, schools, transport, etc. The group watches for births, marriages and deaths and takes along flowers with an appropriate word from the church on the label. It watches for illness and need and offers whatever help it can practically – taking a pie for dinner, doing the washing or cleaning, looking after the children for an hour, just calling in or whatever is appropriate.

At the meeting they share information about contacts (in strict confidence), plan further help and pray for them. They also pray for four or five homes in a street so that over a number of meetings all the homes in their streets are covered. The meeting then ends with a Bible study covering an aspect of witness, caring or social action so that the members grow in awareness of their neighbours and of their mission toward them as the Body of Jesus.

The Watch and Pray Group begins slowly but after a time it becomes impossible to pass a neighbour in your street without speaking to them and the Group becomes deeply involved with the life of the neighbourhood in Jesus' Name and in Jesus' Spirit.

Group excercises

See Appendix 3 for a survey form and hints on using it. Each member of the group, using the same form, survey twenty homes. Agree your roads first so as not to overlap. On one form make a synopsis of the information you have gleaned from the other forms. Discuss your survey visiting and the facts emerging from it. What conclusions can you draw? What action should you take?

What methods of evangelism would be most fitting for your area?

Can you now plan to use one or more of the methods described in this chapter?

Chapter 11: The Use of a Christian Home

Christianity was born in a home. It was in the upper room of a home that Jesus met with His disciples for the last supper. It was in a home that the Holy Spirit came upon the first apostles and 'filled the whole house'. This may well have been in the same upper room for after the ascension of Jesus 'they returned to Jerusalem . . . and when they had entered they went to the upper room where they were staying' (Acts 1: 12–13). It is probable, that this is the house of 'Mary, the mother of John whose other name was Mark', (Acts 12: 12) where Peter so surprised the prayer meeting after his miraculous release from prison.

Homes continued to be used for Christian meetings of many different kinds: for the breaking of bread (Acts 2: 46 and 20: 7–11); for teaching and preaching (Acts 5: 42 and 20: 20); for prayer (Acts 12: 12); for evangelism (Acts 10: 22 and 16: 32); and in the last chapter of Acts we find Paul in Rome in 'his own hired house' to which people 'came to him at his lodging in large numbers. From morning till night he explained to them his message about the Kingdom of God, and tried to convince them about Jesus' (Acts 28: 23).

As Christianity spread across the gentile world, homes were again used as meeting places for the groups of Christians. There were churches (fellowships of believing people) in the houses of Priscilla and Aquila at Rome (Rom 16: 3–5), Gaius at Corinth (Rom 16: 23), Nympha (or Nymphas) in Laodicea (Col 4: 15) and Philemon in

Colossae (Philemon 2). Other groupings of names or the phrase 'and all who are with them' may also cover other house churches. The normal place for meeting was in a home. Not until the time of Constantine did Christians have church buildings and this only because they replaced the temples of other gods. In turning from homes to church buildings there may have been some advantages to gain but there were certainly great losses. Stephen Neill comments, 'The gospel must be brought back to where people live, in simple forms and in terms of small manageable fellowships'. Let us now turn, then to some ways of using our homes for Jesus.

The home as an outpost of mission

John Goddard,[24] in one of his lectures on Christian education points out that every Christian family has a great network of connections that should be natural channels for the communication of the love and care of Jesus and of the gospel. The father has those he works with and travels with, his friends and contacts. The mother has friends she meets shopping or seeing the children to school, the neighbours, some of whom she may have in for coffee and other contacts. The children have their friends at school and in the neighbourhood and through clubs and other interests.

The average family of four has forty good contacts through this network that could provide natural and genuine openings for sharing the faith. Every connection is one that Jesus can use if it is bathed in love and prayer.

When our three boys were small, we had family prayers at breakfast as many Christian families do. But when they got to teenage years they were so full of different interests and pursuits (from the early morning paper round for pocket money to clubs, groups and homework in the evening) that we never seemed to be able to be 'all with one accord in one place' at any one time. So we talked it over together and decided we would put Thursday evening aside as a family home evening come what may. It meant being ruthless but Thursday evenings were blocked out in our diaries as a time to be together. Whether we talked, played games or just watched the 'telly' was unimportant. What we did we did together.

One hour of the evening would be spent reading a Bible passage and sharing in turn what God was saying through it to our lives and our situations. Then we would talk over any family concerns and then go on to think about our neighbours in the road. Were any lonely or ill that we should visit or bring flowers from the church? Were any in need of a word of encouragement or a loving notelet or of prayer or of particular help? We planned necessary action and prayed for them. It meant that every morning we got up, pulled the curtains and looked out on the road in which we lived, we did so with pastoral care in our hearts and saw our home as a mission outpost of the church.

In Liverpool we met a Christian teacher who had been brought to Jesus through a boy from a home like this. The boy was walking home from school and found himself beside the teacher going the same way. The teacher talked and asked the boy what he was going to do that evening. The boy replied that it was the evening for family Bible study and prayer. The teacher was surprised and asked the boy whether it was 'any good'. The boy witnessed very simply but frankly about the presence and work of Jesus Christ in his own life. What the boy did not know was that God was already at work in the life of the teacher who was restless at heart and looking for real meaning and purpose in life. The teacher began to come to the boy's church and soon became a strong, witnessing Christian.

Hospitality

Loneliness is the great modern disease and it affects more people than is apparent. There are many people dulled, depressed or dying inside for want of an encouraging word or a touch of loving warmth.

It was Thomas Merton, speaking of human love in courtship and marriage, who said, 'It is when another recognises in us infinite value, in spite of the fact that we see ourselves as worthless, that it is possible for us to be created anew'.[25] That is so in a much wider application. It is true of what Jesus did for us. It is true of even the simplest touch of a Christian upon the life of another who feels insignificant or of no worth inside.

Hospitality, even asking someone in for a cup of coffee or a meal, is such a touch. Some Christians have a gift of hospitality (1 Pet 4: 9–11) and can use it greatly. Others we have known ought to leave any great gestures in this field strictly alone. They have a definite ungift for hospitality! They worry for a fortnight before anyone is coming for a meal. What will they think of the home? What about that worn piece in the carpet? Will they notice any dust? Should I get my hair done before they come? When the visitor comes they are far too worried to relax and enjoy the company and fellowship and for a fortnight after they worry themselves to death about whether they 'did it right' or what the visitor noticed or thought.

If you are one of these people then find some other way of caring and sharing. Hospitality is definitely not for you! But most of us can use our homes for Jesus by giving hospitality in a simple way. We can have people in to coffee or a meal or an evening together – the widow up the road, the shy young person or the nearby couple who don't seem to make friends with others. Many are reminded of a heavenly Father not because we bring the subject up in direct conversation but because we give thanks before a meal, or because there is a text on the

wall which speaks to them or, above all, because of the
atmosphere of a home in which people love one another
and Jesus is present. Never try to create an opportunity
to speak about Jesus but pray for sensitivity, guidance
and for 'God's appointments' and always take an opportunity if it comes naturally and rightly. Some people
really want to know about God. Some are not yet ready
and we do not press but we do pray. Molly, as she told
in a previous chapter, was brought to the end of 'religion'
and to the beginning of a new life in Christ by the
hospitality of a home. She saw Jesus there in the lives
of others and became hungry for living bread.

Home Bible Groups

Mary was a young married woman in our first church
and she and her husband moved to Surrey, a wealthy
part of the country often called 'the gin and Jag belt'.
But there they found no lively Christian fellowship. They
travelled ten miles into Guildford to worship but were
deeply concerned for their own village.

Mary visited every home in her road saying, 'I am
starting a coffee-morning and Bible study every Tuesday
at half-past ten. Would you like to come?' Now Mary is
a girl with a big and loving smile and lots of enthusiasm.
Six ladies came to the first morning. Within a few months
the numbers were up to twenty and the group was
needing to split into two.

The Bible study followed coffee and was very simple
but a very definite challenge as the ladies faced what the
Bible said and what God asked of their lives. Some very
remarkable conversions resulted without any kind of
pressure except that of the Holy Spirit speaking through
the Word of God. In groups such as these argument is
out and so is theoretical discussion or the swapping of
opinions. The only two basic questions for a Bible group

are 'What does the passage say?' and 'How does that apply to my life?'

For churches setting up home Bible groups we would warmly recommend *How to Conduct Home Bible Classes* by A J Wollen.[26] It is simple, basic and is the sort of material that avoids the kind of discussion that is a good game for middle-class people but which does not change hearts and lives.

Home prayer groups

One of the things that has thrilled our hearts in recent years is the rise of prayer groups and prayer triplets. Again and again in churches that have known revival we have traced back the beginnings to a prayer group.

There is the Baptist church in Poynton which at one time was down and almost out. It had eleven members on paper and less in attendance and a decision was made to close it down. But five old ladies who were members there felt that this was not what God was saying. They began to meet regularly for prayer for revival.

God, almost immediately, began to speak to a man named David Pringle, a lecturer in a teacher training college a few miles away. The thought began to turn in his mind almost like an audible voice – 'Go to Poynton'. David knew about Poynton but it was not his church and he felt no inclination in himself to go there. But the inner voice persisted and at last he wrote a letter to the secretary of the church offering to come over and help them. The church secretary received the letter but saw no point in pursuing it. The church was going to close. After waiting a week or two for a reply, and getting none, David Pringle got on his bicycle and went across to Poynton. He found the little old church building in the High Street, went round the side and discovered a door open. Going in he found the five ladies praying for revival and he quietly sat and prayed with them. When the prayer was over he explained who he was and said, 'I believe God is calling me to come and help you at Poynton'. The reply was immediate, 'Come on then. What's stopping you?'

David Pringle and his wife Ann came to lead the cause at Poynton and they brought with them such love and joy and great expectation that the church grew rapidly. Today it is a lively and flourishing church with a large new church building with a coffee-shop open on one side and a Christian bookshop open on the other. But it all began with five old ladies in a prayer group!

Similar stories could be told of prayer groups from Somerset to Fife or from Hertfordshire to Buchan. In Peterhead, the centre of the white fishing fleets, a visiting preacher quoted a prophecy that Europe would experience a time of social and moral decline 'but Britain would be saved by praying women'. This so struck the women of Peterhead that they formed home prayer groups. The blessing that has followed has been moving and continuous.

Prayer triplets are a particular kind of home prayer group where three people meet together at any time and in any place convenient to them. Each has three people whom God has laid upon their hearts for prayer so that nine people are being prayed for at each triplet meeting. Prayer triplets were an important feature in Mission England and in Scotreach (a three-year mission programme for Scottish Baptists), and some wonderful things happened as a direct result of them. The story of their beginning is told in Brian Mills' book *Three Times Three Equals Twelve*[27] and help in setting up prayer triplets can be obtained from the Evangelical Alliance.[28]

Film evenings

A church with video equipment can use homes in a relaxed way to present the gospel or introduce a discussion on Christianity. Invite friends and neighbours and when you have six definite acceptances invite also six loving Christians from your church – the kind that can relate well to your guests, make good relationships easily and can speak of Jesus naturally and genuinely. When all are there and introduced show a Christian video, perhaps one of the shorter Fact and Faith Films[30] or something from Trinity Video[31].

At the end of the film bring in coffee and biscuits promptly and ask what people thought about the film. It is an excellent opportunity for the Christians to share a personal testimony and to witness through friendship and personal sharing. Non-Christian homes can also be used where the occupants are willing and interested. Robert Scott-Cook, a church planter in the Bristol area, has used this method to great effect.

Parties

If you have families within the church who love parties and who live in an area where parties flourish, this will be a good channel of witness. However, it is sometimes wise to call them 'evenings' or 'at homes' because the word 'party' in some circles suggests that the guests should bring a bottle of alcoholic drink with them and that will not be helpful!

The couple in whose home the party is to take place should visit friends and neighbours in the road, inviting them personally couple to couple as well as giving a written invitation to remind them of time and place. Seek six definite acceptances and invite six Christians from the church as well.

Near Christmas a carol singing evening goes well. If the home does not have a piano then someone with a guitar or other means of music is needed – even a cassette player will do. After twenty minutes of chat to introduce people you simply sing half-a-dozen of the old favourite carols. But each is introduced with a very few words about the message of the carol, or who wrote it and why (there are some good stories here) or explaining a difficult line in the carol (such as 'born to give them second birth'). After six carols everyone is thirsty and in comes the coffee and biscuits over which the Christians present, suitably seated among the guests, open up conversations about carols and their message or Christmas and its meaning. This can provide an evening that everyone enjoys. No-one has preached at anybody but the gospel has been simply and clearly presented.

Near Valentine's Day have a Valentine evening with games, recitations, songs and readings all around the theme of love. Include (without comment) a good reading of 1 Corinthians 13 and 1 John 4 verses 7 to 21 and George Herbert's poem 'Love bade me welcome'. The last game could be that of giving a paper and pencil to every guest, asking them to write 'Love is . . .' and then to complete the sentence. Then everyone reads what they have written. Both here and in the later personal chat over coffee the opportunity is given to share testimonies about the love of God in Jesus or to say what difference He has made to our home and relationships.

Birthday parties can be happy occasions for inviting non-Christian friends and neighbours. After a hilarious evening of good, clean fun everyone yells for a speech from the one whose birthday it is. He has opportunity of thanking everyone for coming and of thanking God for the past year, perhaps giving a very short testimony of some particular experience of God's guidance or blessing.

In November and early December book evenings go well. Get a good supply from a Christian bookshop and portable shelves. Pick the books you would particularly like to get into the hands of people in the neighbourhood – good Christian stories and biographies, *Mere Christianity* and others of C S Lewis's books for the intellectuals and plenty for children. Invitations go out widely. People can come in and out and can browse and buy or not buy as they choose. Coffee and biscuits are available all the time (without charge but ration the biscuits to any boys people bring with them!) Every fifteen minutes a book is introduced in one minute by someone (holding it aloft) saying what it is about, reading a paragraph or saying what effect it had upon them.

The training group

In our first church we found a group of people keen to learn how to witness and we were keen to learn with them. We therefore set up a house group we called 'The Fish' which met every week. We all wore a silver 'fish' badge and if asked about it were pledged to witness to Jesus as well as we were able.

On the first Tuesday evening of every month we had a Bible study with an emphasis on witness. We used selections from John's Gospel and Acts seeing how Jesus and the apostles dealt with particular people and situations. On the second Tuesday we went out in pairs visiting old and lonely people. The people expected us and welcomed our pairs warmly and our visitors soon lost their fear of visiting and began to enjoy doing the job with thought and care. Some read the Scriptures to those not able to see well themselves or took a picnic tea to share (and took away the dirty dishes afterwards). All visits ended with a simple prayer – we sent them nowhere where a prayer would not be welcomed. Both visitors and visited were blessed and this later gave birth to the great three-year area visitation in which the whole church became involved.

The third Tuesday was to discuss questions people ask. Members of the group brought questions they were actually asked at work or elsewhere and we discussed ways of answering them. The fourth Tuesday evening was witness evening when we told of our contacts and conversations during the past month, discussed how to develop better approaches and simpler language and prayed for our contacts.

We also tried various experiments to discover people's reactions to tracts and literature in order to find out what best touched people.

The squash

In our training group, 'The Fish' we made use of any fifth Tuesday of the month by holding a Squash. As it was held in one room of a home and at one time over thirty people came, it was very literally a squash! Members of the group invited all the contacts of the past month to a discussion on Christianity.

The evenings began with a short prayer that God would help us to be open and honest with each other. Then an invited speaker would talk quite directly about Jesus and what He did and promised. This lasted not more than ten minutes.

As soon as the talk ended Molly and two helpers would wheel in a trolley of coffee and cakes. Everyone was quickly served and the trolley disappeared so as not to interrupt again. The chairs were already arranged in groups of four with a Christian leader planted in each well before the meeting. He would begin by asking 'What did you think of the speaker?' If the answer was favourable he would ask what points they agreed with most or what points had challenged them most. If unfavourable he would ask what points they disagreed with particularly. Whatever the response the conversation was on Jesus and the Christian life. The leader's job, having set the ball rolling was to ensure that everyone in their small sub-group had a chance to share and that the sharing was kept on a friendly though open and honest basis. Other Christians in the sub-groups were able to share their testimonies and sometimes it was a new convert who made the most memorable contribution.

We had some communists and some atheists who came to the squashes but there was never embarrassment or difficulty on either side. It was an open and honest evening during which neither Christians nor non-Christians felt inhibited from contributing freely and honestly. The evening began at 8.00 pm and we usually had to eject the last sub-groups, still talking keenly, after 11.00 pm. These squashes were the means of conversions as well as happy and direct encounters.

Conclusion

Your home belongs to Jesus. He has given it to you to use for Him. Now let your imagination begin to work on how you could use your home for Him.

A couple in our second church had a small boy. They also had a calendar which had a page with a text for every day. The little lad had claimed it as his right and privilege to tear off the previous day's page every morning when he got up. One morning his mother was putting a note out for the milkman and the lad followed suit by picking up the calendar page and putting that also under a milk bottle on the step.

A little later the milkman rang the doorbell and, holding up the text, he said 'Do you really mean this?'

'Why?' asked the mother, 'What does it say?'

The milkman read it out to her but, not being familiar with the Bible, he put in a comma where no comma should have been. He said 'It says, "Walk in, love"!'

If we truly walk in love in the Spirit of Jesus it will mean that our doors will be open to all kinds of people and we will welcome them in with a warmth that reminds them of Him.

Group exercises

1. Share experiences of any home group evangelism in which you have been involved and the lessons good and bad you learned from them.

2. Are there any methods mentioned in this chapter you could now plan to use?

3. 'Church buildings are useful as a cover for the weather but they also keep church people in and non-church people out. Worse they breed a mentality that sees witness only in terms of running or going to organisations. They can destroy the personal and keep us from the work that God really told us to do.' Discuss this quotation. Where have church buildings some advantages and where have homes their advantages?

4. Why do you think Christianity has progressed so fast and so well when it has not had church buildings (e.g. in its early years and more recently in China)? What should we learn from this?

Chapter 12: Visitation Evangelism

—

What we say when we witness to Jesus is not so important as what we are – and this applies to church witness as well as to personal sharing. Many evangelistic efforts fail because a poorer spirit or meaner motives show through the fine words we speak.

We are constantly asked, 'How can we get people to come to our church?' The very question shows a wrong understanding of both the church and of our witness. The only answer is to tell them to stop trying to entice people into church premises and instead to let love and prayer flow out toward people because the outgoing love of Jesus is beating in our hearts.

Let's stop the spirit of 'in-grab' and let God's love pour out. Let's stop inviting people to meetings and begin to share the life and Spirit of Jesus. Let's stop asking 'How can we get them in?' and ask, 'How can we let the care and beauty of Jesus shine out?' Where He is lifted up He does His own drawing in.

Many 'campaigns' we have seen have not been campaigns at all but just wild raids across the non-Christian border. Student missions can be like this unless they are carefully prepared for and truly part of the ongoing mission of the local church. Some 'visitation' we have encountered has been no more than pushing bills through people's doors – the church equivalent of the children's trick of ringing the bell and running away! We have been invited to speak at evangelistic rallies but when we arrived we found only church people there.

The church folk were perplexed. 'But we took out eight thousand leaflets,' they say, 'Why haven't people come?'

An impersonal leaflet means nothing today. We get far too many through our letter-boxes anyway.

What is needed is first a lovingly attractive fellowship, with members out there in the community living such lives of love, joy, peace, forgiveness and generosity that Christianity is both seen and felt as a viable option to others. There is a need for Christians to get to know the people of the neighbourhood at depth. We need to know and befriend people – and not just to invite them to the next evangelistic rally. Befriend them because Jesus loves them and your life is open to Him and to them to be a channel of that love, rally or no rally.

Visitation is one way of both getting to know your neighbourhood and of letting the love of Jesus be felt. It is a good method anywhere except perhaps in small villages.

Sometimes church people say, 'We cannot do visitation. The Jehovah's Witnesses and Mormons do that here'. Yes, that is why these cults build up large congregations. There are people out there who want to find God. Don't leave them to the cults to pick up.

Let me describe four methods of visitation:

The survey (See Appendix 2)

This is simply a way of gathering information. (If you do not intend to learn from and use the information do not do a survey.) It also helps those doing the survey to lose their fear of visitation and helps them feel what makes people tick in your area. Apart from the information received, the fact of having met and listened to so many non-church people will have brought a deeper understanding and compassion for them. This is where true witness is born.

There are two objections that are raised to doing a neighbourhood survey. One is, 'We don't need a survey. This church has been here sixty years and we all live in the area. We know what it is like'. In fact surveys often show that what church people believe about their neighbourhood is either well out-of-date or based on sheer illusion. One minister of a city centre church told us, 'No-one lives here any more.' The figures showed that one thousand people lived within five minutes of the church building but they were tucked away in flats above shops and round back alleys. Another church told us, 'This area is now full of Asians'. We discovered that it was in fact twenty-seven per cent Asian – far from 'full of Asians' and that even there the Asians were predominantly gujarati speaking and tracts in that language were published by the Bible Society. It helps to get the facts straight first.

The second objection is, 'Why should we do a survey? The Holy Spirit will tell us what to do'. Our trust in the leading of the Spirit of Jesus is strong but it does not take away the need of our own careful effort and enquiry. In the work of the church there is God's part and we cannot do that. There is also our part and God will not do that. It is God who gives the rain and sunshine, God who gives the increase but He will not dig my garden for me while I sit idle. Surveys are to help us do our part intelligently and well, so that we do not hinder the Spirit of God in His work.

The information you get from a survey is largely a clear picture of the way people feel – a big and important factor in your approach to them. For more concrete facts about the neighbourhood and its needs see the local social workers and others. The council will also supply further information, especially about future projected developments. Basic information can be obtained from the Offices of Population, Censuses and Surveys. Ask for their Small Area figures and for an explanation of them. These will cost you less than £5 and are a mine of information.

A small group of suitably gifted people within the church should then be given the job of sifting all the information received and presenting the relevant pieces in simple form. Suggested forms for a neighbourhood survey and a church survey are in Appendix 2.

The direct challenge

As the best example of direct challenge visitation we will describe the method called 'Evangelism Explosion'[31] recently renamed 'Teach and Reach'. When it first came to this country from America we were somewhat sceptical of it. We looked at the 'diagnostic questions' ('Suppose you were to die tonight and stand before God and He were to ask you, "Why should I let you into heaven?" What would you say?') and thought them quaint. 'Great for America,' we said, 'but not the kind of thing for Britain'. But we have been proved totally wrong. In so many churches – especially those with a good fringe of partly interested people – this method has been greatly used.

The method is taught in 'clinics' – courses set up in different parts of the country. They are expensive but very helpful. They teach door-to-door evangelism by groups of three Christians. They are taught first to make a rapport with those they are visiting by asking and showing caring interest in their daily life and then in their church background. If and when the time comes to present the gospel it is given in a pattern which the presenters have learned off by heart. The pattern is:
1. Grace. Heaven is a free gift. It is not earned or deserved.
2. Man. Is a sinner and cannot save himself.
3. God. Is both merciful (He doesn't want to punish us) and just (He must punish sin).

4. Christ. Is the God-Man. His death paid for our sins. He lives and offers us heaven as a gift we may receive by faith.
5. Faith. Is not mere intellectual assent. It is trusting Jesus Christ alone for salvation.
The Christian witness is then trained to lead a person who is ready to a sound commitment to Jesus Christ.

The presentation can have the danger of leading people to the gift rather than the Giver but the course has set thousands of people free to witness, has given them a pattern to follow and has been used of God to bring thousands of non-Christians to a real knowledge of Jesus.

This method sends out visitors in teams of three which allows one or even two of the team to be apprentices learning skills for future small team leadership. It is therefore adapted to continuous evangelism and not just to the quick campaign.

Visitation and home groups

The best example of how to go about this is given in a booklet called *Good News Down the Street* by Michael Wooderson.[32] Michael Wooderson was in charge of a church in a large new housing estate. He had studied the Evangelism Explosion approach and learned from it but saw an initial need to discover interested people and to seek invitations rather than barging in.

He first sent out any church members who were willing to visit every house in the estate making friendly contact and, where it was not inappropriate, to ask 'Would you like to find out about God?' When anyone expressed serious interest the visitor would ask them to fix their own time and evening and for six weeks running three people from the church would come to that home so that they could all find out about God together by looking at the Bible. The householder was told to invite any relatives, friends or neighbours who would like to find out about God. They all did so – not one of them was going to be sitting there on their own facing three people from the church!

The six week course was simple. They looked at Scripture passages on such themes as 'Who is Jesus?'; 'What did Jesus do?'; 'Jesus is alive' and 'What it means to follow Jesus'.

During six years two hundred people received a visiting team of three and worked through the course in their own homes. Five did not complete the course. Fifteen were already Christians. Forty made no positive commitment. Four made a commitment some time after the course. But the remarkable fact is that 136 people made their commitment to Jesus through the course and most went on to become members of the church.

Gavin Reid, writing of Wooderson's method, says, 'Why has this approach been so effective? We must start by giving first place to the work of the Holy Spirit through the course, those visiting and in the meetings. Prayer plays a large part. But when all this is agreed, I believe we must say that those who followed Michael Wooderson's approach got a number of things right.

1. They were sensitive to people
2. They sought out the seekers – the people ready to find out about Jesus.
3. They had a flexible approach so that they could keep going continuously without exhausting the resources of their small church.
4. They used lay power – eighty-nine different combinations of church members, using 150 people in all, went out in the first six years.
5. They used people's homes
6. New converts were immediately trained and went out with the teams as apprentices, giving no time to become lukewarm.
7. Their approach was natural and relaxed – no 'sales patter'.
8. They built relationships as they talked together. (This

holds the secret of why so many of those visited actually joined the church and stayed – they started with at least three good friends there.)

9. And, yes – their simple course was centred on Jesus.'

Relaxed and in homes, chatting and sharing over six weeks (not a 'one-off' shot) and in a company wanting to find out about God and sharing together simply over the Scriptures – here is something fundamentally right. We commend it.

The Mission of Friendship

One effective form of visitation evangelism is the Mission of Friendship.

1. The aim

It is to be clearly understood that the Mission of Friendship is simply one step in the perpetual mission of the church. The minimum aim is to make a deep and caring contact with the people of our neighbourhood, to build up goodwill towards the church, to witness to Jesus genuinely and naturally and, when opportunity offers, to help people to commit themselves to Jesus as Saviour and Lord.

The final aim is, however, much wider. It is a total involvement in the needs of the whole area in order that we might be as yeast in the meal and to win the whole area, in its wholeness, for the Lord. In this method we are not seeking to perform a social service nor merely to win a few souls into an individual relationship to Jesus. We are seeking to follow the pattern of the incarnation, to become involved (in the Saviour's Name and in His Spirit) in the needs of body, mind and spirit of the whole neighbourhood.

Do you know Kipling's poem, 'Mulholland's Contract?' In it the tough Mulholland of the cattle boats tells us how he was converted during a storm at sea and made a contract with God:

> An' by the terms of the Contract, as I have read the same,
> If He got me to port alive I would exalt His Name
> An' praise His Holy Majesty till further orders came.

But the word of God that came to him was different from that he expected. It was 'back you go to the cattle boats an' preach My Gospel there'. Mulholland says:

> I didn't want to do it, for I knew what I should get,
> An' I want to preach religion, handsome an' out of the wet.
> But the Word of the Lord were lain on me, an' I done what I was set.

These same orders are given to us: to get back to the life and to the neighbourhood in which we belong and to claim it all for Christ.

Just as the little band of disciples in the early days set out with the incredible vision of the world won for Jesus, so we must (if we share anything of His Spirit – John 20: 21, 22) set out with the same love and joy in our hearts to claim our home, our street, our neighbourhood, our job, our fellows and our community for Christ. This means an identification, in His Name, with people in all their joys and sorrows, their successes and their sordidness. Working through us will be the same challenging, winning and divisive Saviour, still calling people to Himself and still serving us in the same Spirit and with the same love, whether people accept Him or not.

As that great pastor-evangelist, Tom Allan said, 'In this kind of mission the volunteers have to be prepared to undertake a long and arduous task which will involve them in heartbreak and disappointment, and compel them literally to get their hands dirty in the business of the parish'.[33] It is not easy to love in this way. Unless the love of Jesus possesses our hearts we shall not be able to keep it up. God is not only going to use us for the blessing of others: He is going to teach us what it means to be a Christian in the world today. It will mean blood and toil and tears and sweat. It will mean walking with Jesus against the whole drift of the world's security-seeking, comfort-seeking and selfishness. It will be sharing the glory of the crucified.

We who so tenderly were sought,
Shall we not joyful seekers be?
Celestial Seeker, send us forth!
Almighty Lover, teach us love!
When shall we yearn to help our earth
As yearned the Holy One above?[34]

2. The method

Christians engaged in the Mission of Friendship go in twos. Those willing are given some thorough but simple training beforehand. The training is mostly to teach them to depend on the Spirit of Jesus, to relax and enjoy the company of others, to help them speak of Him naturally and genuinely and to give them some practical hints and tips.

The ideal method for this visitation is where all visitors meet at the church building one or two evenings a week and after prayer and encouragement set off to visit in the roads assigned to them. They then come back to report and have supper together. However, there is much to be said for pairs to meet on their own and visit at the time that suits them best. Two ladies, for instance, could well go in an afternoon while the children are at school, meeting to pray beforehand. Whichever arrangement is followed visitors will have a list of names and addresses and when a door opens to them will greet the person by name. (This checks the information they have and allows the church computer or card-index system to be kept up-to-date. The names come in the first place from the electoral roll, Kelly's Directory and also from members.)

It will be agreed beforehand which one of the visitors will speak first. It is usually wiser for one to lead and to bring in the other at the opportune time. After the first greeting the visitors introduce themselves as from the church (or churches) and say they have come on their Mission of Friendship. This is the point where the reputation of the church in the locality counts for everything. If it is a church with a reputation for loving care then people will be glad they are calling. The reputation is something you earn. They then begin to ask questions which show a genuine interest in the other, beginning with such obvious questions as 'How long have you lived here?' If they are asked in they accept with pleasure.

It is ideal for church members committed to this type of visiting to be set free from other church commitments but, in busy churches where this is impossible, you can give each couple only three visits a month to make. Wherever couples make good contacts they are given the same name to visit again – and again. The idea is to cultivate deep and genuine friendship in Jesus' Name and Spirit. This will mean that progress is slow but that does not matter. Slow progress is usually the best progress. It may well take three years to get round the whole neighbourhood once. And by then it is time to begin again for a quarter of the people will have moved.

A regular visitation (yearly or three-yearly) of those who are open to visiting is good. The church becomes known and thought of as a caring body. After each visiting time every pair makes out a report on the visits they have made, and talks over the visit or visits, discussing how they might improve on their approach or procedure, and whether they should do anything further to help the particular family or families. They then spend time in loving prayer for them.

The report (given to someone in the church who coordinates visits and follow-up) gives information such as:

a) The name and address of person or persons visited.

b) Details of others in the home and ages of children.

c) What church background they have.

d) Suggestions as to whether another visit by the same couple is required, or by another couple, better matched in interests.

e) Whether the household visited is in need of practical help, and if so, what?

f) Any other information you feel you should give.

All information is, of course, to be kept in strict confidence and not gossipped about.

Our fears in visitation

Recently we were training a group of forty people in visitation evangelism, and we asked them to put down what hindrances they felt. When collated thirteen hindrances were named – and eleven of these were things within ourselves! Most of them began with 'Fear of . . .' – fear of doors being slammed in our face (an extremely rare occurence unless your approach is brash), fear of what people will say, and so the list went on. Perhaps we need to go back to the foot of the cross to learn and receive again that perfect love that casts out all such fears.

Let us deal with the top two fears in visitation.

1. Fear of being asked difficult questions

Some worried Christians (an incompatible phrase) ask, 'What shall we do if they ask us questions we can't answer?'. Our reply is simple. Just say, 'I'm sorry I don't know. If it would really make any difference to your life I'll find out. In the meantime let me tell you what I do know'. Let it be relaxed, genuine and fear all gone. We are called to be witnesses, not walking encyclopedias.

165

2. *Fear of hostile people*

Hostile people are few but it is always possible that you will call the day after the minister of St Cucumber's has run over the family cat! Whatever happens, stay sweet. If you can't cope at all, apologise for calling and go. But it is far better to listen with genuine care and interest to what the hostile person says! After all, it is only our pride that can get hurt and it will not do us any harm to give that up. Our human reaction is to respond to hostility with hostility but that is not the way of Jesus. There is a story told of a Christian who went to buy a paper and the paperman was, for some reason, quite rude. A friend said to him, 'That man was quite rude to you. Why were you so polite to him?' The Christian answered, 'I could not choose what attitude he would have toward me, but I could and did choose what attitude I would have toward him'. In fact he let Jesus choose.

If you have listened with real concern – caring more about what is 'bugging' the other than about yourself – you will quite often find that after an outburst of hostility an irate person will sober down and begin to tell you his or her story, sometimes defensively and sometimes apologetically. It may be that he says that a churchgoer sometime in the past has done him an injury. It may be more in his own mind than real but listen, sympathise and add 'that wasn't Christian at all'. That gives you a chance to talk about Jesus and what *is* Christian.

If he runs down the Church – or your specific church – don't defend it heatedly. Admit that the Church is composed of weak and often erring human beings like ourselves whose whole hope is in the mercy and forgiveness of Jesus and in His work of love in our lives. Say what God has put in our hearts to do in this mission and why. Our business, like the Lord's, is to strive to turn enemies into friends.

When we do meet a hostile person it is good to recollect the words of Jesus when He sent out His disciples

166

'as lambs among wolves'. He told them to offer His peace to every house and when that peace was rejected He promised 'your peace will come back upon you' (Luke 10: 5–6).

We have rarely met hostile people. But how wonderful to know God's peace coming back upon you as you do.

Group exercise

1. In a group, consider the following (mythical) report made by Miss Vera Vinegar and her colleague Donna Cara Rapp to her minister, the Rev Hope Little, after they had been on evangelistic visitation. Consider each paragraph in turn saying where Vera and Donna went wrong.

'We visited Mr and Mrs Bloggs and we knew as soon as the door opened we had made a mistake. He had a red nose – obviously a drinker – and she was not the type we want at our church at all. She probably goes to bingo. They asked us in although we didn't really want to go and offered us some stewed tea which, of course, we refused. We sat on the hard chairs. We had to insist on it. The armchairs were not at all nice. I expect they had fleas in them.

It was gone ten at night by the time we got to them so I got straight down to the business of asking them if they were saved (we knew they weren't) and told them they must be born again. That shook them, I could see. They looked quite stunned.

We talked at them for about half an hour and then left. I have discussed them with one of their neighbours since who told me they had a child in hospital but we didn't have time to talk about their personal details at the time. We just wanted to get the message over and get out. I didn't like Mr Tosh's attitude. He kept saying, "Gor Blimey" and before we left said "Wot d'yer fink God's got ter say t'a man loike me?" I don't like sarcasm and told him so. We should never have gone there. I have always said this is a hard and indifferent area. People are not interested in God and being respectable. All they live for is the pubs and the pools, the bingo and the television. Nothing good comes out of that.'

Chapter 13: Hints and Helps for Door-Knockers

We will try to summarise here some of the training helps we give to groups embarking on visitation of the Mission of Friendship type.

The initial approach

When as a pair you receive your assignments, unless times are already fixed, discuss and agree when you will visit together. Be thoughtful also for the people you are visiting. If, for instance, you are visiting an old lady who lives alone, then go in daylight. In any case do not call on people after 9 pm (except by appointment). It might also be wise to avoid times of popular radio or TV serials they are likely to hear or watch. Meet, read carefully over any information given to you, agree who is to make the opening remarks at the first door (some pairs do so alternately but if one is an apprentice he will do so only when he feels ready) and commit yourselves and your visit or visits into the mighty hands of God.

Go dressed in neat, ordinary clothes and not your Sunday best. Remember people may be having a look at you through the lace curtains before they open the door. It will not do to look like visitors from the cults or like the bailiff's men! You will probably have literature to take. Know it well. Have also a pencil and notebook in your pocket and a torch if you will need it. Take only a note of the names and addresses you are to visit. Leave information slips at home but read and memorise them well. Go together with prayer in your hearts. Make sure you have the right name and address and then knock on the door. This is often the worst moment in any visit and you will be tempted to hope no-one is in! Here again breathe a prayer for the people. (Don't kneel down on the doorstep, of course, or it may prove too much of a shock to the one opening the door!) Stand a little to one side (a 'non-threatening' position), prepare for adventure with God, recall the promise of Jesus to be with you, that the real work is that of His Spirit and relax in His love.

When the door opens, smile. Remember that the person before you may well be more nervous of you than you are of them and a smile will help you both. Say, 'Good evening. Mr Smith?' and when he acknowledges that he is the man you want, carry on something like this: 'We are from the Whateveritis church. We are visiting the neighbourhood on our Mission of Friendship and have come to say we care about you and to bring you this message'. Here hand over your literature and a friendly covering letter. Some people will immediately ask you in and you will, of course, accept with pleasure.

When you have visited a few houses you will begin to relax and feel a little more confident and may be able to pick out people to whom, when you say you are on a Mission of Friendship, you can add, 'May we come in and tell you about it?' If you are cheerful, friendly and open you may often be asked in.

However, for the moment we will suppose that you have handed in your literature and are still on the doorstep on your first visit. What you will say next will depend to some extent on what response you get from Mr Smith and there is no steroetyped pattern. If there is little response you will want to show further caring interest by asking simple questions such as 'How long have you lived here?', 'Where do you come from originally?' and so on. It may well be that you experience the fulfilment of the Lord's promise 'It shall be given you in that hour what you shall say'.

It may be you will find, almost before you begin, that you have called at an inconvenient moment. A man who has had to answer the door in the middle of bathing the dog (the rest of the family having very wisely gone out) is not always in the best mood for friendly chat! If the time is wrong for any reason whatever, apologise and try to make a definite appointment to call again. If there is any trouble in which you can be of help, you will of course stay and do what you can but if you are just in the way, bid them a friendly farewell and go. A following visit made by appointment is often a good one. People feel they now owe you their attention and want to explain about the difficulty they were in when first you called. If you are willing to listen well and express sympathy and understanding, a friendly relationship is established at the outset. One possible response when you have handed over the literature from the church is 'How much is it?' (Lord, have mercy upon us for our reputation as those who always want money!) This will provide an excellent opportunity not only to say it is free but to explain just why we are engaged in this Mission and how God has an outreaching love for people that can change their lives for ever.

If there is little response, it will be the time to ask questions that show personal, caring interest. Simple questions (like 'Have you settled well here?' or 'Have you made good friends in this neighbourhood?' 'Where did you come from originally?') can quickly get people talking, often establish common links and do make a relaxed and friendly feeling. Once people get over the shock of finding that a church really cares about them, most are glad and willing to begin sharing themselves.

These are general suggestions. If you have found a way of approach which is more natural to you and equally effective in making friendly dialogue, then use that.

You might see some easy means of contact out of the circumstances of the visit. You may notice that the man is a keen gardener, can congratulate him on it and, if you are keen on gardening too, say a word or two about your garden. You may notice that he has just painted the front door and can congratulate him on a neat or colourful piece of work. (Don't let him see the paintmarks on your coat – you can remove those later!) Be guided by the Holy Spirit as He works through your own particular commonsense and friendliness and through the circumstances of each visit. No two visits are exactly the same. The method of approach is that of offering friendship and this often has three steps. The first is always the offer of your own friendship in the care you show. The second is the warmth and friendliness of the church which you represent and to which you will certainly introduce some. The third step is that to which our care and prayer is aimed – that they might find the transforming friendship of Jesus for themselves.

There may be some visits in which you will find people in whose hearts the Spirit of God has already been working – some who are actually ready to become Christians. These instances are comparatively rare (on average every 240 calls) but they do occur and these people are a joy to lead into a personal relationship with Jesus.

But the slow, step-by-step way will be the normal progress of things, continuing to visit and build up an open, sharing and caring friendship with those interested. Better to be slow and keep the doors open than rash and brash and find all the doors closed to further contact. It may take many visits to establish enough trust and care to be able to talk openly and directly about spiritual things in an effective way. Four, five or six visits would be normal to get to a direct, open stage.

Before returning to a house spend time together thinking and praying about the people lovingly and about the objectives of this visit. The most important thing is that our care for people should be genuine and not just bait for our hook. A pretence at Christian love will neither do nor endure. We are not going out to make our congregation bigger and our church 'successful' nor from personal pride or feeling of superiority. We are going because the love of Christ compels us. The most untalented of people may find an entrance into the hearts and homes of others by real Christian love manifested in warm-hearted friendliness. The happy intercourse of personalities is the very essence of true living and there is nothing so interesting or rewarding as a real care for people. It is the fruit of the Spirit of Jesus and the heritage of every Christian. With this, too, goes the ability to listen to other people's points of view about life. I remember our philosophy tutor back in college days saying that the important thing was not merely to know what others thought (he was speaking about some of the Greek philosophers at the time) but to understand *why* they thought it. In our seeking to befriend others in the Name of Jesus we shall have to learn the same secret – not only to hear what they think but to place ourselves with them in a sympathetic spirit, to feel their lives, their hopes and longings, their fears and troubles, and to win the right to share our hearts with them – opening the door for Jesus to come in right where they are.

Down in the human heart, crushed by the tempter
Feelings lie buried that grace can restore;
Touched by a loving hand, wakened by kindness,
Chords that were broken will vibrate once more.

(Frances Van Alstyne)[35]

The art of conversation

Conversation is important not only as a means of giving information but also as a means of making warm contact

173

between persons. A good deal of ordinary conversation carries very little information. To take an obvious example when two ladies meet in the street in the teeming rain, one says, 'Isn't it wet?' and the other replies, 'Yes, isn't it?' This kind of interchange conveys nothing they did not both know before and looks silly when repeated in print. But the two ladies find it quite happy and adequate because they have shared a little warmth of fellow-feeling.

We have always found visiting a happy part of our work although also tiring. It was said of the Lord when the woman touched the hem of His garment that 'power went out from Him'. And when we go out in His Name to identify ourselves with the needs and troubles of others, we shall often find something of the same thing happening to us. We are giving not only of our care, our interest and our attention; we are giving of ourselves. The art of conversation is simply the art of being truly interested in people and things. It is helpful to be informed about things of topical and general interest and this means an intelligent reading of the daily news and of the local newspaper. You will also need to keep an eye open for evidence of people's hobbies and interests.

I remember visiting one man from whom I got little response until I asked him if he had an interest in any sport. He immediately perked up and said 'Cricket'. Now cricket is a game which interests me little. It is far too slow. I am therefore somewhat ignorant of its fortunes and heroes. However I had heard on the television of the preparations for the test match at that time, so I asked, 'What do you think of our chances for the test?' We then embarked on a long conversation in which I said very little but 'Yes' and 'No' and 'Do you think so?' but I learnt a surprising amount about cricketers and tests matches and we parted like old friends.

People like to talk and to share their thoughts and opinions on the things they have studied and there is always a place and a welcome for the interested listener.

Should you get a cricket fiend in your visits, listen well, establish friendly contact and next time take with you a keen Christian who is also keen on cricket and let a new friendship be formed to share the love of cricket and the love of Christ.

When you are asked into a home make a friendly gesture right at the start by saying a word of gratitude and by praising anything that you find interesting or appreciate (the cosiness or neatness of the house, a picture or a vase of flowers). This must not, of course, be an affectation. You should be genuinely aware and appreciative of 'those things that are good and deserve praise'.

In some homes you will find a television set on – perhaps loudly. Some homes have it as a permanent background to their living and take little notice of it. The suggestion that you hang your coat over the TV set is not one to be followed! If there is a programme on in which all the family are interested and it is coming toward its climax it may be as well to sit and see it with the others. Normally you can sit close to the person you are speaking to or even ask if you could have the set turned down. If it is one member of the family, or the children, who are watching then you will be able to talk quietly to the others in another part of the room – or go into another room. If the situation is going to be too difficult make an appointment to call again.

Usually when people ask you in they will make you at home. Then relax and enjoy their fellowship. Don't bore them by doing all the talking (when nervous we are inclined to talk too much!) but encourage them to talk, and listen with interest to all they have to say.

You will find most people woefully ignorant of the gospel and unaware of their own ignorance! All the same when false statements are made do not contradict them aggressively and dogmatically. Share your own experience lovingly or say 'I'm glad you raised that. Jesus . . . ³

175

and go on to say what Jesus said or did and add 'It does make you see things in a new way, doesn't it?'

It may be helpful to reply 'Do you know, a year ago I would have said exactly the same thing but I will tell you what made me change my mind – in fact it changed my life . . .'

If a statement is made which is a partial truth then appreciate the positive piece and begin, 'That's a good point and there is another thing we ought to say too'. Then add the full truth. Tact and appreciation of whatever good there is in the other man's point of view is the best way of ensuring that he will listen to yours.

Dale Carnegie advised us to get people saying 'Yes' as much as possible before we put the important questions. Far be it from us to employ the tricks of successful manipulation but it is the positive things we share which will provide the ground for the new things we have to say.

Whatever happens never argue. From argument comes only the hardening of attitudes and sometimes bitterness and anger. You are there to win the man, not the argument. As you talk, try to see things from the other person's starting place. Avoid religious phrases and talk in language he will understand. Dr Sangster had an amusing paragraph about this in a book published some time ago called *Let Me Commend* (Epworth Press). He talks about the war years and says: 'In the long years I lived in air raid shelters, I recall hearing one night a good woman, much addicted to pious phrasing, speaking to a tramp for the good of his soul. The conversation had been proceeding some little time when it fell upon my startled ear. Fragments of her speech floated over the blast wall. She was saying, ' . . . I suspect you are still living under the old dispensation . . . I am not sure you understand the difference between natural and effectual faith . . . You do realise, don't you, that all your righteousness is as filthy rags?. . . .'

The tramp took little part in the conversation. When

finally she left him, murmuring something about 'interceding for him at the throne of grace', he found himself again, and just said as she went (not jeering but vaguely aware that she meant to be kind) "Okey dokey". I felt that two worlds had met in those two persons – and they had not intersected'.

We must also avoid the Pharisaic spirit. The visitor who raises his hands in pious horror because the other drinks, smokes, goes to nightclubs or to bingo, is not likely to get very far along the way of friendship.

I remember going into a house where the host immediately opened the drinks cabinet and offered me 'a touch of something'. I do not drink alcohol on principle but I recognised his gesture of friendship, thanked him for it and simply chose an orangejuice. It was done in a way that accepted his friendliness although not compromising my personal principles and we were able to sit down to a good talk together. In fact he became a Christian as a result of our sharing about Jesus.

Sometimes people will try to avoid the challenge to their hearts and minds by bringing up secondary things like behaviour patterns or denominations. Often it is not so much conscious and intentional as an instinctive defence mechanism of the mind. An outstanding example of this is in the story of the woman at the well in John's gospel (4: 3–42). When she found the challenge getting too uncomfortable for her she tried to evade the issue by turning to a nice little argument about where people ought to worship or by shrugging off everything by saying, 'Well, when the Messiah comes we will know these things, won't we?' Each time Jesus brought her back gently but surely to an encounter with God or with Himself and His offer of new life. This must be our aim also. When people attempt to sidetrack the real issue, bring them back to face Jesus. You can spend a great deal of time arguing about football pools or church procedure or some other issue but it is time wasted. The centre of Christianity is not in a set of rules or in ritual but in a living fellowship with Jesus Christ. It is not something but Someone. When people come to accept Him and His Spirit and purposes into their lives then secondary things are seen and dealt with from quite a different angle and always in relation to Him and His Lordship.

If questions are asked to which you do not know the answer, say so frankly. If they are genuine problems say you will try to find out the answer, and do so. You will learn in doing it. It can be helpful to ask 'Would it make any real difference to your life if I found the answer to that?' Where the discussion or problems are too deep, take along someone suitable in both knowledge and Christian spirit who can discuss more deeply with the other. Books like *Mere Christianity* by C S Lewis[36] do provide an intellectual approach and can be bought cheaply to give or lend to others.

If people criticise other churches or ministers, simply express sorrow to hear of any trouble, acknowledge that all of us have our failings and need God's mercy and forgiveness and tactfully change the subject. Do not condemn or run down any other denomination or person. It is not helpful, it is not polite, it gets spread around and it does damage to relationships. Do not outstay your welcome or stay too late. When the time comes say how much you appreciate being with the people and, unless you feel it is not suitable, ask 'Can we pray together before we go?' It is rarely that this is refused (when it is, drop it without demur) and if the prayer is short, simple and loving then it is usually warmly (sometimes movingly) received. Just thank God for the home and the happy time you have had together, for the blessings He has given us and commit the people, each one, and any concerns they have shared into His mighty and loving hands.

When you get home you will give the required details on your report card but otherwise remember that all you have heard is confidential and is to be mentioned only to your minister and then only if it is going to be for further help to those you have visited. If you have had a happy time, why not write a short notelet thanking the people for their kindness to you. It is a little thing but can mean much to others. And if you have made promises of any kind do make sure they are carried out.

Do not be discouraged if on many visits you do not get further than the first step of establishing a tentative friendly contact. If you go in the Spirit of Jesus and with His caring love within your heart the most ordinary conversation will reveal something of Him and will prepare people to hear more.

> Not merely in the words you say,
> Not only in the deeds confessed,
> But in the most unconscious way
> Is Christ expressed
> Is it a very saintly smile,
> A holy light upon your brow?
> Oh, no! I felt His presence while
> You laughed just now.
> For me, 'twas not the truth you taught,
> To you so clear, to me so dim,
> But when you came you straightway brought
> A sense of Him.
> So from your life He beckons me,
> And from your heart His love is shed,
> Till I lose sight of you and see
> The Christ instead.

Leading a person to commitment

I remember my old college principal saying, in answer to complaints that students were not trained to have a set answer to every situation that might arise, 'You can't train students in that mechanical way. You say, for instance, "How should we deal with a drunken man?"

but there is no such thing as a drunken man. There is Mr Smith when he is drunk and he is quite different from Mr Jones when he is drunk. And Mr Robinson when he is drunk on beer is quite different from Mr Robinson when he is drunk on whisky. In the one instance he may be docile and drooling and in the other, fighting mad'.

It is true that there is no stereotyped way of dealing with a drunken man and neither is there any stereotyped way of dealing with people seeking for God. As we have said earlier, some patterns (like the *Four Spiritual Laws* or the Evangelism Explosion pattern) may be most helpful to know and use as the opportunity requires but they must never become rigid steps which we demand that the seeker must take to count himself as one of the elect. Christianity is not an assent to a set of intellectual propositions, creed, or series of statements, even though they may be from Scripture. Christianity is Jesus. Both creed and statements can be helpful but they arise out of, and cannot take the place of a living encounter with Him and the daily walk of fellowship with Him in trust and obedience.

Likewise, the Scriptures testify about Jesus and are the very footstool to His throne but they were not given to be marshalled into a series of propositions for mere intellectual assent. The Christianity we take forth is not just the communication of information but the communication of the divine life, transforming existence from within, and this is the work of the Holy Spirit. It is not our view of the Bible or of the atonement or of anything else that can save people but only Jesus Himself by His Spirit and in His own love and power.

Further, people come to Jesus for very different reasons. Not all come with a sense of sin. Some come seeking for a purpose in life, some looking for meaning and integration, some for the great friendship because they are lonely, some for forgiveness for they are guilty. Others come from worry, unrest, an undefined sense of something missing, from fear, because of the appeal of goodness and beauty, the attractiveness of Jesus seen in the Scriptures or in Christians. All these things and more can bring people to the Saviour, and, whatever brings them, His promise remains true, 'Him who comes to me I will not cast out'.

There are some who have come for the selfish reason that they want the blessings of heaven and to escape the horrors of hell. God does not reject them because of their selfish aim but in that loving, patient way of His He takes and teaches them of His own great heart until they love Him for Himself and not for what they can get and their hearts begin to beat with the purpose, care and generosity of His Son as they look upon others and the world around.

We cannot foresee what will happen on our visits but it is likely at some time (it could be on your very first visit) you will meet with someone with whom God has been dealing and they are just waiting for an opportunity to be shown The Way. When you find such a person, express your pleasure and let them tell you their own story in their own way. Listen with warm and attentive sympathy and when at last it is your turn to respond, begin right where they are and with their particular sense of need. Whatever their need point them to Jesus. He and He alone is the final answer to all the needs of the human heart. We were made for Him and we find our rest in Him. Without Him desire must ever roam and rule our hearts. Without Him, as He said, our lives become like dried up and withered sticks upon the ground (John 15: 6).

If you have been talking to someone who is very near to commitment, and they are not ready there and then to make their decision, make an appointment to see them again soon and leave them a booklet. Get them to agree to read it, to think about it and pray about it. And pray for them yourselves. Maybe you should get a prayer triplet or a number of people to pray for them. Often when you return you will find they have made their commitment on their own in the interval.

When people are ready to make a commitment of their lives to Jesus, His people and His purposes, use the way customary in your church. It may be by using the 'clock' page and prayer in the *Four Spiritual Laws* (Appendix 5). It may be by signing a decision card. If so make sure it says what they want to say and can sign from the heart. You will pray with them. It may be that their commitment will be by way of a prayer. Some are quite ready to pray. Others find it difficult and it is a help if you pray first, telling God about them and asking for His forgiveness and cleansing and His gift of new life in Jesus. If it is still difficult for them to pray let them pray a simple prayer, sentence by sentence, after you, including a clear repentence and a full commitment. Then you pray again, thanking God for Jesus and all He has done for us, for all His promises and the certainty of their fulfilment.

We will speak more of caring for the new convert in the next chapter. This is of vital importance. However, immediately give him or her a modern translation of Luke or John and get them to read and ponder a paragraph each day, to listen to what God says through it and to ask how it applies to their life. They should also pray about it and talk to God about everything, growing in trust and obedience and in likeness to Jesus.

There is joy in the presence of the angels of God when one sinner repents and you will find great joy and a great stimulus to your own Christian life when you have been used to lead someone else to Jesus.

The contents of this chapter are reduced to a simple list of hints and tips on visiting in Appendix 3. The list may be reproduced without infringing copyright but should carry an acknowledgement.

Group exercise

If your church is embarking on a visitation campaign, invite all interested to read the above chapter and then use the Witness Simulation Game in Appendix 1. What have you learned?

Chapter 14: Care for the Convert

John Calvin asserted that for those to whom God is Father the Church must be Mother.

As is often said, Jesus did not tell us to make converts. He told us to make disciples. A disciple is a convert who is growing to maturity so that he knows what the Scriptures teach, is able to apply them to every part of his life and relationships and is able to share the faith with others. Jesus places the new convert into the hands of the church to be nurtured and taught. 'Teach them' He said, 'all that I have taught you' (Matt. 20: 20). The teacher's task begins, not ends, when the pupils have enrolled.

The recruiting sergeant is not content simply to enlist people. He enlists them to be trained for arduous service. The builder does not simply collect together the materials but builds them into a house. And God is building a house in which He is to live by His Spirit (1 Cor 3: 16 Living Bible).

'Edifying the Church' (i.e. building up the church) is one of Paul's main themes. By grace you have been saved, through faith, but not simply to be one in a collection of saved individuals. Now you are *fellow-citizens with God's people and members of God's household, built on the foundation of the apostles and prophets with Christ Jesus Himself as the chief corner-stone. In Him the whole building is joined together and rises to become a holy temple in the Lord. And in Him you too are being built together to become a dwelling in which God lives by His Spirit*.

We go wrong if we confine our work *only* to helping individuals to change – repentance, faith, prayer and Bible reading, church attendance and so on – important though this is. God's purpose is that we come to maturity as we enter, live and relate within the living fellowship which is the Body of Christ. This is the aim of church leadership – not just to provide religious services and maintain a building but to draw Christians into those deep and strong relationships with one another that makes them the Body in which Jesus lives and through which He is seen and felt by the world.

Church members are to be closer together than the stones cemented together in the temple wall. They are built together as the parts of a Body: each member exists for the life and good of the others; each is needed by the others; each is dependent on the others. 'God Himself has put the Body together in such a way . . . so there is no division in the body. . . . If one part of the body suffers, all the other parts suffer with it; if one part is praised, all the other parts share its happiness. All of you together are Christ's body and each one is a part of it' (1 Cor 12: 24–27).

The convert without a church background

Today an increasing number of converts and those beginning to attend churches have not been to Sunday school in their childhood and have gained no knowledge of Christianity from religious education in schools. They come from a totally secular background and need to begin a lot further back than was necessary in past days. Such people are best helped at the beginning on a one-to-one basis, preferably with the Christian who brought them to Jesus. If that Christian feels inadequate they can associate another loving and sensitive Christian with them and make it a threesome. Where there are two converts who are of similar background or interests a 'bud' group (of three to five people) will serve the same purpose.

The aim is to have simple sharing sessions over selected Bible passages on particular themes. Call them 'Bible readings' or 'Bible sharing' – words like 'study', 'class' or 'training' are generally unpopular.

These sessions are informal and are best when taking place in a home. They begin with a time of personal chat, then a short prayer for God's guidance and blessing and a reading of a short piece of Scripture. There follows a personal and open sharing by each of what God is saying to them through those verses and how it applies to their lives (home, work, relationships, habits, attitudes) right now. The older Christian applies the passage honestly and openly to himself, not to the new convert. It must be recognised that the teacher is the Holy Spirit through the Scripture, not the older Christian, though he can help in any passages that cause difficulty.

We would normally suggest five sessions of this kind covering the following topics and references:

1. Assurance (John 5: 24, 6: 35–37 and 47).
The first person to visit the new convert the morning after his conversion will be the devil. He will be saying to the convert, 'You didn't really mean it, did you?', 'You don't feel any different, do you?', 'It can't really be true, can it?' If you are the one sharing with the new convert you ought to be there promptly on the same day to read what God says about assurance.

The new convert needs to know that his salvation does not depend upon his feelings (which may go up and down with moods or events) but totally on what God has done in Jesus Christ and in the promise of His own Word. This is vital.

2. Prayer (Luke 11: 1–13 and 18: 1–14).
The convert will have noticed that prayer is just talking to our heavenly Father about anything and everything

that comes our way. He will need to learn also that prayer is not telling God what we want but bringing our lives and everything in them and daily laying them at His feet for whatever He wants. It is here we listen as well as speak and seek His spirit, guidance and purpose.

3. Scripture (2 Tim. 3: 15–17 and Luke 6: 46–49).

It is probable that by now the convert is reading the Bible for himself. If not, after this session get him reading daily, either with beginner's notes or beginning with Luke in a modern translation and reading a paragraph a day, pondering it and applying it to his life and living. The important thing he is learning from you as you share the Scripture is to listen and to hear God speaking through it and then to obey Him.

4. The Holy Spirit (Rom. 8: 12–39).

The convert needs to learn that he is never alone and never needs to fear to carry out whatever God tells him to do. The Holy Spirit is there to make Jesus real in our lives, to enable us to do whatever Jesus wants and, through all, to make us like Jesus.

5. The Body of Christ (Col. 3: 8–18, Rom. 12: 1–21).

The convert must understand that he is not born again only into an ethereal or individualistic relationship with Jesus but is born into a new family, and is a member of the Body of Christ.

These five sessions assume that the convert already knows enough about Jesus to have made a sound and genuine commitment. They are only 'tasters' but should start the new convert off in the right direction.

The nurture group

The new convert who lacks a church background should now be ready for a nurture group of eight to ten people, some of whom are new converts and some loving, sensitive Christians who are happily and easily able to share what God is saying and doing in their lives, at the same time standing on the same level as everyone else in the group. However, converts with a good church background and knowledge of spiritual things may well begin straight away in the nurture group without the preliminary personal Bible sharings.

The new convert should ideally join the nurture group accompanied by the Christian who led him to Jesus who will then be a fellow member of that group but this is not always possible or advisable. The importance of the nurture group to the new convert cannot be overstressed. Nurture groups are powerful things. Wrongly understood and handled they can be highly divisive. Properly understood and well run they help Christians grow to maturity at a fast rate and bring depth, life and creative relevance to the whole church. The nurture group gives a sense of belonging, support and pastoral care and at its centre is personal sharing. *It is not a teaching group and does not need a teacher.* No one person sets out to teach the others. It is simply a group which allows itself to be led and taught by the Holy Spirit through the Scriptures. It is also a group where people can talk about what they are learning, understanding and practising.

Teaching is, of course, needed in the church and this is best given in sermons or in large groups taught by someone with knowledge and the gift of communicating it. But this needs to be balanced by the small group which goes on from gaining knowledge in the head to applying it in everyday life and sharing in the life of a group of apprentices to Jesus.

So many of our members agree with every word that is said and sung on a Sunday but when they step out on

Monday morning they are at a loss to know how to apply their faith and feel completely on their own. The small group studying, applying and sharing how the Scriptures are working out in their daily lives provides the supplement and balance needed. Life today is increasingly impersonal and institutionalism in the church keeps us busy but often at the cost of genuine meeting and loving, relational fellowship and mutual support. Much of this comes from a misunderstanding of how people learn. Parents sometimes come to us and ask, 'My child is now a year old. How can we begin to teach him about God?' The only reply is that the parents have been teaching the child about God and about life from the moment he or she was born. From the first moments the baby has been drinking in relationships, attitudes, reactions and values from the parents. The atmosphere in the home, their treatment of and attitudes to each other, to neighbours, to crises, to things and to people have been fundamental teaching that has gone deep within the child's being long before his or her parents begin to 'teach' anything verbally. In fact one Christian psychiatrist has said, 'A child has learnt half of all he will ever learn by the age of two-and-a-half'.

It is in the same way that the new convert learns about God and about the Christian life, spirit and attitudes. What is preached from the pulpit will have very much less effect than what is preached by the fellowship of the church. A lukewarm, individualistic and impersonal fellowship will produce lukewarm and shallow church attenders. A deeply supportive and sharing Christian group will grow deep, loving and effective Christians who know what they believe, can apply it to all life and can share the faith with others.

It is often hard for churchgoers of the respectable, 'stiff upper-lip' and 'Christians have no problems' type to begin sharing in a small group. They would rather hide in a personal pietism that demands little. Those who do join small groups, like aspiring athletes beginning to train, find it can be hard and painful at first. All sorts of undiscovered spiritual muscles ache and pride has to be surrendered to Jesus. But finally they begin to enjoy it and become glowingly fit.

Nurture groups begin slowly. Most begin with the fear, 'I am afraid to tell you who I am, because you might not like who I am and I am all I have to give'. But as the weeks go by the masks begin to come down bit by bit, fear diminishes and the love and acceptance of Jesus begin to rule. Then members find themselves hearing the Word of God in a new and living way and increasingly knowing the presence and guidance of the Holy Spirit as they share and practise that Word. To be a member of such a group is a complete education for a new Christian.

At one time we stayed in the same church for three weeks which is unusual for us. Our work usually means a one-week stay with any church and we are off again (some of our friends say that after we have been in a church for one week we have to be off again!)

We stayed with a retired couple and the man was leader of the house group in that home. He was a dear man but not of the type you normally associate with leadership and efficiency. He was more like everyone's favourite uncle. We wondered how he would manage a house group but we were in for a surprise. He had been simply but thoroughly trained and led his group superbly. They used Navigator material and were in the middle of the course called 'Design for Discipleship' (see Ch. 15). The group had a good inner discipline. They had each read a portion of Scripture every day (as the course booklet directed) and had filled in a one-sentence answer to a question asked. The question was personal and concerned the application of that passage to our own life and living. The leader, Bob, opened the group on time by asking one of the members to pray. He then read the question that had been allocated for the day following the last meeting and each of us in turn read what we had written in answer. This was repeated for each of the seven daily readings and sometimes members would add to their answer by giving an account of the situation, feeling or event that had prompted their answer. It was an open sharing of what God had been saying to us through the Scriptures during the past week and was most warm, honest, and moving.

One of the group was a new member. He had come because his wife was a member of the group and was coming home each week so full of joy and excitement he felt he was missing something. He was not a committed Christian but was open to learn. Our first meeting was his second and he was still shy at sharing what he had written in case it should sound elementary or naive to others well advanced in Christian life and knowledge. But Bob beamed upon him warmly, giving him worth by his look, and when he had shared Bob thanked him for his honesty or insight.

During the three weeks we were there that man visibly grew into commitment and into biblical Christian living. It was heart-warming to see.

Bob's group had adopted pledges at the beginning and one was of pastoral care for one another. No member of that group was ever ill, in need or missing on a Sunday or from the group meeting but several others would be on the phone or at their door to see if everything was alright or if they could help. They had learned to love one another deeply. One of the members of that group told me, 'We have learned in this group that fellowship is sharing. I believe that any member of this group would willingly lay down his life for another member'. That group had developed strong 'family' bonds.

One of the couples in the group had two teenage boys. While we were there the younger of them had taken his brother's car, without permission, and gone off joy-riding in it. He came off the road on a bend, went through a field fence and the broken fence post went through the front of his neck, severing the jugular vein.

By the grace of God there was a policeman nearby who knew exactly what to do. The lad was rushed to hospital, and, again, there was the surgeon who could deal with his urgent need.

When the police phoned the parents they immediately phoned Bob who rang the rest of the group. All prayed for the boy and for his parents and every evening at visiting time members of the group were at the hospital bed. The nurses pulled the curtains round the bed while the group prayed quietly. The hospital staff were deeply impressed with the instant support and loving care shown and the parents were carried through their agony by the love of the group. They were told that the boy would live but would probably never be able to speak again. But one day the older brother went in to visit and the injured boy not only pleaded for forgiveness with his eyes but tried to say 'sorry'. It was only an attempt – but the voice was there and he finally recovered completely.

'When one member suffers, all suffer,' says Paul, 'and when one member rejoices, all rejoice'. We had seen that in practice in the support this group gave to the parents and their erring son. That should be ordinary and natural everywhere within the Church. It is best developed in home groups and it should be the experience of every new convert.

Content of nurture group learning

A course for new converts ought to be mainly post-baptismal (or post-confirmation) so that the Christian life is seen to begin, not end, in conversion and baptism. Such a course is best of a year's duration so that group life has time to go deep and learning and sharing in a group become a natural part of the Christian's life. That cannot be done in a few weeks. It is a long-term business to nurture and wean a babe in Christ until he is a mature member of the family of God, living a committed Christian lifestyle and able to win and disciple others.

One part of the need of the new convert is to know the Christian faith – what the Bible teaches and what we believe. The other part is to see and understand how to apply that faith and Spirit to his daily life – how to live it out on Monday.[37] These two aspects cover very many topics, such as:

The Christian life
1. What is the gospel?
2. What is a Christian?
3. Assurance
4. Biblical principles
5. How to pray
6. How to read the Bible
7. Worship
8. How God guides us
9. How to deal with temptation
10. How to keep in fellowship
11. How to witness
12. What discipleship means
13. Christian behaviour
14. Christian citizenship
15. The stewardship of all life
16. The ministry of every member

The Christian faith
17. Knowing God
18. Jesus, the Christ
19. The death of Christ
20. The Holy Spirit
21. The Trinity
22. The Church
23. Baptism and the breaking of bread
24. What is man?
25. Sin
26. Repentance

27. Forgiveness – God's and ours
28. Grace
29. Faith
30. Love
31. The Kingdom of God
32. The last things

Our denomination
33. Its principles
34. Its relation to other denominations
35. What church membership means

Other points on the Christian life
36. The problem of suffering
37. The Christian in God's world
38. Christian lifestyle
39. The fruit of the Spirit
40. The gifts of the Spirit.

These topics will fall into five series of eight studies, although in fact quite a number of them cannot be completed in one week and a topic like the Christian in God's world will open up many other topics like war, race, environment, use of resources and so on. Other topics may give rise to discussion about such things as the Christian's responsibility in a society with a high level of unemployment or violence, and extra time will have to be given to this.

Each study should be prepared for by every member of the group. The best way to do this is by issuing a list of seven Bible readings, some simple but basic questions (the kind that lead to sharing and action, not to theoretical discussion) and perhaps a few basic notes. The members of the group will have read and meditated on one reading a day and thus will have done quite a bit of simple preparation for the group meeting. (It would be good if every church expected to do such Bible reading and preparation for every Sunday service. The minister is expected to prepare – and gets so much rich blessing from preparation – and both the people and the services would be benefitted if the members did too!)

Let us here stress three important points for the new convert that should come through all the study/sharing:

Discovering Jesus in His Body

We stress that our fellowship with Jesus is a very personal thing. That is right. But it is not an individualistic thing. An individual is one who stands on his own. A person is one who stands always in relationship with other persons, (in fact in a great and complicated network of relationships with God, with all other persons and with all creation). When we are baptised into Christ it is not just our body or an ethereal 'soul' that is baptised but our whole life, home, work, attitudes, values and all our relationships. This we begin to learn as we share together in the group and experience the blood bonds of Jesus Christ binding us together in His Body and purpose. There we begin to experience the life of Jesus as part of the life of the Trinity. As the Father ever pours out His life upon the Son so we, in Him, share in that life. As the Son ever gives back His life in glad and loving obedience to the Father, so we, in Him, share in the giving of that obedience which is faith. And the Spirit is the moving life of it all. That is why togetherness is always an essential and central part of the Christian life and experience – because our God has togetherness in the nature of His Being. So we cannot truly worship or serve or know Him without togetherness.

Some of Jesus' hard words come to mind here. As, when His mother and brothers came seeking Him, He said, 'My mother and my brothers are those who hear God's word and do it' (Matt. 12: 50). In other words, the Christian family is to know ties deeper, more wonderful and precious than even the deepest natural

196

family ties (and in Jewish families these were deep). Again, Jesus makes it clear that if we cut ourselves off from a Christian brother or sister we cut ourselves off from Him (Matt. 5: 15).

The idea of every convert having a mature Christian who is a spiritual 'cover' for him is a good one if the 'cover' is a loving and humble elder brother. But where the covering is of any kind of authoritarian nature it is not only non-Christian (Mark 10: 42–45: 'It shall not be so among you,') but prevents true growth to maturity in the new convert. We would much prefer the loving responsibility of the group for one another, which has its own discipline and authority but totally within the bounds of love in which each puts the others before themselves and prays, loves, serves and ministers each to all for the good and growth of all. There is only one Lord and that is Jesus. There is only one law and that is agape love. We stand, live and grow together in His grace alone.

Discovering the world

As we study the Bible honestly in the group and share and relate it to our daily living, we begin to discover Jesus in the world. We begin to see our life and daily experience and all creation as the sphere of His presence (in grace and judgement) and the sphere of our ministry in and to Him.

Martin Luther has a great sermon on vocation (our Christian calling). He says that by virtue of his baptism every Christian is ordained to ministry. And that ministry covers every part of his life. If he is a married man, his first sphere of Christian ministry is to his wife. And if she is a Christian her first ministry is to her husband. Each is given a charge to minister to the other as deep and as serious as the charge given to a minister being ordained to minister to God's people. God will hold each responsible for the other. That transforms our understanding of marriage.

Second, if the Christian is also a father he has a ministry to his children. He and his wife are given a little private missionfield of love and are called to teach the children by living out the Jesus-life and love before them in every attitude, response, relationship and value.

Third, if he is an employee, he has a Christian ministry to exercise toward his workmates, toward his employer, towards his trade and towards the public he serves. That is not easy today but God has not ceased to give us this charge.

Fourth, he has a ministry as a neighbour. Every morning when he gets up and draws the curtains he is to say, 'This is the field of my/our ministry. God has put me here to minister to my neighbours. By love, prayer, caring service, listening, hospitality and help I will be a channel of God's love and grace to them in every aspect of my life'.

Fifth, he has a ministry as a citizen of his town or country to live for justice and freedom and stand against wrong in Jesus' Name. Sixth he has a ministry as a member of the world; a ministry as a steward of creation. All this we learn both in our heads and in our sharing experience as a group.

Discovering our gifts[38]

Every Christian has a gift or gifts. They are given by God to be used for His glory, to fulfil His purposes in and through His Body. The church's job is to help every member discover, develop and use his gifts that the Body might be alive in every member.

No one member can do everything, but everyone can do something. What he is to do is indicated by the gifts God has given to him. The last two or three meetings of the new converts' group should concern spiritual gifts.

The passages to study are Romans 12, 1 Corinthians 12–14 (don't separate the teaching of 1 Corinthians 13 from the rest), Ephesians 4 verses 4–7 and 11–16 and 1 Peter 4: 7–11. Then give everyone a piece of paper and let them write down on the left side of the sheet the names of everyone in the group (including their own). Then against each name ask them to write what gifts they perceive the person to have (remembering that the gifts God gives are not confined to those mentioned in the New Testament). The papers are then collected by the leader (they are now anonymous) who reads to each person in turn what others have written as his or her gifts. If the group has been sharing at depth for a year it is surprising what perception and consensus of opinion has developed. This is one of the best of several ways of discovering the gifts of members.

When the initial (one-year) group for new converts is ended it is good to encourage every member to join two new groups, meeting alternate weeks. (We would happily see this form replace the old church structures and multitude of non-productive meetings.) The first would be a geographical group of the Watch and Pray kind (see chapter 10) responsible for the few streets in which the members live. The second would be a gift group – all those with the same gift joining in a group (or groups if there are more than twelve). Those with a gift for evangelism, for instance, would meet bi-weekly to share their work and experiences of the last two weeks, to pick up insights and understanding on how to evangelise the area better. They would pray for contacts, sometimes have further training, study the Scriptures on witness (especially John and Acts) and plan their work for the next two weeks.

Conclusion

There is no doubt that the key to the life and continued growth of Christianity in its early days was not only in the winning of converts but the life and presence of the Holy Spirit in the community of believers, making a fellowship in which the life they shared together was the life of Jesus, giving depth, love, loyalty and a faith that laid every part of life wide open to God. It is this we need to recover. Any teaching we give to the new convert will be academic and without context unless it becomes alive in the new community of Jesus.

In this home groups are fundamental not only for new converts but for the ongoing life and ministry of the local church. In our next chapter, therefore, we will look further at home groups in the church.

Note: We need to be careful about those we call converts. In a recent mission a claim of 330 converts was made. That was the number who came forward in response to the appeal. Many were children and some had no clear idea of why they had come. Less than twenty went on to nurture groups and church membership. These alone could truly be called converts.

Group exercises

1. Read Luke 6: 12 (and Mark 3: 13–14); 8: 1; 9: 1–2 and 10: 1–6. Do you discern any training pattern here? If so what? What kind of training was it? What should we learn from it?

2. Do you feel the church is called by God in this present time to change the life and history of the world? Do you feel you have a significant part to play in God's work? If you are to play a significant part, what further training do you feel you need?

3. Each use the Discovery of Gifts form at the end of Appendix 4. Share your top score and affirm and encourage one another.

Chapter 15: Home Bible Groups

From the day of Pentecost believers commonly met and 'had their meals together in their homes, eating with glad and humble hearts, praising God, and enjoying the good will of all the people. And every day the Lord added to their group those who were being saved' (Acts 2: 46, 47).

Up to the time of Constantine the Christians had no church buildings as such and home groups continued to be central to the nurture and spread of the faith. In the New Testament there is the frequent mention of 'the church which is in their house', (Rom. 16: 5, 1 Cor. 16: 19, Col. 4: 15, Philemon 2 etc). and the phrase 'and those that are with them' probably refers to further home groups.

Groups have always to a lesser or greater extent been a feature of Christian life and fellowship. They became central to the work of John Wesley and were the main reason why his work flourished and endured. Today they have sprung into prominence again partly because of smaller families (the Christian families of a hundred years and more ago were groups in themselves!) and partly because of the impersonality of modern life which has affected the Church itself. There are some churches today where Christ may be preached but He is not met and experienced in the fellowship or His life and love demonstrated to the world about. But people come to church not for the ritual but to find Jesus present in community. Home groups are helping to restore this.[39]

Kinds of groups

Basically there are two ways of understanding groups. One is by looking at them primarily by their purpose, the other is by looking at them primarily by size.

1. Groups defined by purpose

The Task Group: Exists simply to do a piece of work (e.g. to redecorate the church building). Needs a technical man (eg. a decorator) as leader. The danger to be avoided is not following the leader's instructions or not doing the work.

The Discussion Group: Exists to talk over problems or topics. Needs a keen intellectual or knowledgeable person as leader. The danger to be avoided is not bothering to research topic beforehand sufficiently.

The Nurture Group: Exists to enable Christians to grow in fellowship as the Holy Spirit instructs them through study of the Scriptures and as they share insights and experience. Needs a tactful, loving, avuncular figure as leader who is a good chairman. The danger to be avoided is becoming theory or problem-centred or a discussion group.

2. Groups defined by size

The Bud Group: Two to five people. Excellent for very informal, personal sharing and prayer. Each meeting about forty-five minutes.

The Small or Cell Group: Seven to twelve people (the ideal is eight to ten). Excellent for growth through Bible sharing. Becomes a close-knit family group. Needs the avuncular, chairman-type leader.

The Large Group: Twenty to seventy people. Excellent for teaching. The leader needs to be one with knowledge and the skill and personality to communicate it.

The Congregation (or Celebration as Peter Wagner terms it[40]*):* The bigger the better. Excellent for worship. Needs a leader who is an inspiring preacher.

Each group has its own distinct dynamics and they cannot be confused.

Characteristics of the small or cell group

1. It is formed of seven to eleven people. At twelve it splits into two groups.
2. It meets in a home, relaxed in chairs in a circle, not in rows. The leader's chair is not placed differently to any other.
3. It is not in a teacher-pupil relationship but the group together is concerned with seeking and applying Scripture and sharing insights, blessings, sorrows and experiences.
4. It meets for one and a half hour's work, one hour of which is spent in Bible study and sharing and twenty minutes in praying for members, members' concerns and for the church.
5. A further twenty minutes is afterwards given to tea or coffee and biscuits (no more – any effort on behalf of the host or hostess at giving more lavish hospitality than other hosts is quietly and lovingly discouraged). Everyone should be encouraged to leave two hours from the beginning of the meeting.
6. It must be held weekly or at least every other week. If it meets less frequently continuity is lost.
7. Each group at its first or second meeting should discuss and accept its own pledges on things like confidentiality, regularity, punctuality, praying for one another, pastoral responsibility for and support of one another, reading the same daily Bible reading notes and so on.
8. It is possible for an active group of eight to have pastoral responsibility for another two who are invalids or who cannot or do not want to come to the group.
NB Any church with four-fifths of its members in groups

can give pastoral covering to the whole membership through the group structures.

9. The group is composed of those eager to seek, learn and share and the leader and the method of study used must ensure that all can share with equal willingness and acceptance.

Methods of study for the Small or Cell Group

Basically, with each of the following methods two questions need to be asked about each Bible passage studied and the answers shared honestly and personally.

(a) *What does the passage say? Put it into plain language and terms.*

(b) *How does that apply to my life right now? If I took this passage seriously how would I have to change my life, ways, attitudes and relationships?*

To these questions is added a third:

(c) *How did last week's new light, insights and challenges work out in my life during the past week?*

If we are responsible for and to each other in love the group should be able to ask any member whether he has carried out a challenge he voiced the week before or how a previous insight is working out in his life. Here are some methods used:

1. The Swedish method

Everyone should read and think the same passage through several times in the week preceding the meeting. They place a pencil questionmark in the margin against anything they do not understand, an asterisk against anything which is a new insight to them and they underline anything which challenges them.

At the meeting each in turn talks about what questions arose, and also share insights into the passages. All contributions are received without question or argument

– there is no 'right' or 'wrong' answer – although the leader may have to guide the group to look at other passages of Scripture that cast further light on the passage studied. Next the group shares the asterisks and underlinings and each says why a particular piece is a challenge to him at that moment. The sharing is personal, honest and open though not without sensitivity and tact.

Try this method on passages such as John 1: 1–14; Colossians 1: 9–22; Hebrews 1 or Matthew 5: 17–48.

2. *The rewriting method*

A passage of Scripture is read and pondered and then the members have twenty minutes in which to rewrite as much of the passage as they can in their own words and in terms of their own life situation. Then each in turn reads out what they have written.

For instance, 1 Corinthians 13, might be rewritten beginning thus:

By a doctor: 'I might be able to speak with all the technical jargon but if I treat people simply as cases then I have failed as a Christian. . . .'

By a typist: 'I might be able to type at a rapid rate and show great skill and accuracy but if I do not show loving care for others in the office I work in vain. . . .'

By a businessman: 'If I run a successful business and make much money but do not care for my employees or seek to serve those who do business with me, I do not know what the love of Jesus is. . . .'

By a homemaker: 'If I keep my family well-fed, perfectly dressed and behaved but do not have the Jesus-love that warms their hearts and blesses our home and all who come in it, I am not living the life He wants to give to me . . .'

Try this method on passages like 1 Corinthians 13; 1 John 4: 7–21; Colossians 3: 12–17; or 2 Peter 1: 3–11.

3. The personalising method

A passage of Scripture is read and questions are asked which make the group feel and apply it to themselves. A passage like Mark 2: 1–12 is read and then people write answers to several questions such as:

'How would you have felt if this had been your house and four men had broken through your roof to bring their friend to Jesus? Would you have put your property or the person first?'

'Can you remember a time in your life when you suddenly decided that people matter more than things? Write a little about what you felt and did.'

'Have you ever been carried along to Jesus by other people? Tell of the situation briefly.'

'Is there anyone you can think of who needs to be helped and carried to Jesus at this moment? Could you, or a group decide to do this by prayer and care?'

What is written is then shared in turn, question by question. The aim is to apply the Scripture practically to our own situation and then put it into action.

Try this method with passages like John 11: 17–44, Matthew 14: 22–33, Luke 19: 1–10, Mark 10: 17–31, or John 5: 1–9.

The 'serious' method

Each member of the group, after a passage is read, ponders it and answers the question, 'If I took this passage seriously as a word from God to me now, what difference would it make to my life?' After ten minutes' meditation, each in turn shares their answer.

Some passages possible for this method are:

Philippians 4: 6–8 – Freedom from fear
Philippians 4: 11–13 – Freedom from inadequacy
1 Timothy 6: 7–10 – Freedom from worry
Ephesians 4: 1–6 – Freedom from resentment
Romans 5: 1–5 – Freedom from regret
Romans 8: 28 and 35–39 – Freedom from despair.

There are many bodies issuing Bible study notes or

courses for groups: denominational headquarters, the Bible Society, the Christian Publicity Organisation etc. The Navigators have a series of courses[41] and we have many times used their 'Design for Discipleship' course, although we usually begin with Book 4.

Leadership of Small Groups

The key to the effective small group is an effective leader. He is often not the kind of person we usually think of in leadership terms – not the 'get-up-and-go' person but the 'able to sit down and listen' kind. He is a facilitator, an enabler, a fellow-learner, a good and tactful chairman – a servant in the Lord to the group. *Never start a group without the right, correctly trained, leader.*

Qualities of the Small Group leader
Ideal qualities are as follows:
1. Leaders should be deeply committed to Jesus and to the church, and not likely to take the group off on its own or to seek an ego-trip.
2. They should have a warm and loving personality that encourages others to emerge gradually from behind their masks and share honestly with each other.
3. The leader must have a positive attitude to the Bible and to themselves and should still be growing in Jesus in love, obedience and in every grace.
4. Reliability, trustworthiness, tact and patience are essential and the leader must also have a 'shepherd-heart' that is open and sensitive to Jesus and to people.
5. The leader does not regard himself as the 'teacher' of the group but believes the Holy Spirit will teach through the Scripture as the group meditate and share together and will enrich the group through every member.
6. Any leader will have experience of being a member of a good group and have studied group behaviour and learnt the simple necessary skills.

7. Finally a leader will be entirely helpful to the group and to individual members but will make all more dependent on Jesus, not dependent on himself.

Ministers should not be present in the groups, as too many people regard them as experts and will not open up while a minister is present. The minister's place will be amongst the leaders' group, possibly in charge of it. We will speak of that later.

The Group's first meeting

Unless the members of the group all know each other well, the first meeting will normally be an 'ice-breaking' one. Everyone will introduce themselves over a cup of coffee giving their name and discussing, for instance, their family and the area in which they live. This can be followed by a game that gets people moving and talking to each other. One kind of game is where each has the name of a famous person pinned on their back and they must find out that name by asking everyone else questions – one question per person and Yes and No answers only. In another game you can give a list of interests, characteristics or odd facts about everyone present ('Wears red socks in bed'. 'Always has a kipper for breakfast.' etc) and each member has to find the name that fits each statement. (The statements are collected from members a week before the meeting so there is no embarrassment.)

After the general movement, all come to sit down again. They then ponder several questions (given on a sheet to each) and after four minutes each share their answers in turn. The questions might well be:

1. Where did you live between the ages of seven and twelve and in what kind of family?
2. Who was the most 'warm' person in your life at that time and what is your most warm memory?
3. When did God become more than a word to you and how?

At this point the group can sample their first Bible

study together (have Bibles handy or have the passage printed out on a sheet). Take, for instance, 1 John 4: 7 to 21. Let someone with a good reading voice read it out. Think about it for three minutes and then let each in turn share what God is saying to them personally through this passage. The leader should be first to share – setting the tone of personal application, openness and honesty. No-one is allowed to comment critically on the contribution of someone else.

There will then remain four things to be done:

1. Each can share what their hopes and expectations of this group are.

2. The leader will spell out simply the purposes of the group – especially the fact that they are there to discover what the Bible says and how it applies to their daily lives, not to indulge in theoretical or abstract discussion. He will also explain that the method of study will be by listening to God through Scripture and that no-one is to be interrupted or criticised when sharing what they have learnt.

3. The group should be encouraged to discuss what pledges they would like to make to God and to the group on things like confidentiality, regular and punctual attendance and so on.

4. Full details of further meetings should be given or agreed and homework (usually readings) given for the next meeting.

The meeting can be rounded off with coffee and biscuits.

Further Group meetings

Normal group Bible sharing can now begin. After an opening prayer sharing about a Bible passage will begin – remembering that the basic purpose is to share.

1. What do I hear this passage say?
2. How does it apply to my personal, daily life?

The leader will be the first to share at the early meetings, setting the tone and attitude for the others. At this stage he has to take an active leadership role which will diminish as the meetings go on. He will quietly become less active and take up his real job as servant/facilitator to the group.

The leader's job

The following is a summary of the different aspects of a leader's role.

1. As servant-guide.
He should never press his own opinions or experiences or seek set conclusions but rather encourage others to share.

He should also keep everyone to personal sharing on the passage of Scripture and sharing in love together.

He will ask any person with a tendency to resort to the abstract for concrete examples from their own life of what they say in theory.

He will bring the verbal wanderer gently back and perhaps unobtrusively sum up what he has said that is relevant.

He will take the contribution of the muddler and sum it up gently and clearly.

He will not contradict anyone in the wrong but will ask them to test their thoughts by Scripture and will suggest passages to look at.

2. As gate-keeper.
The leader's role is also to open the gate for the shy or timid members without any pressure on them. He should also help shut the gate for the one who talks too much. This is done, sometimes progressively in several ways.
(a) By the gentle hint: 'Thank you, George. Now let's hear what the others have to share'.
(b) Through steering the conversation deliberately to others. 'What did God say to you in this passage, Mary?'

(c) Through speaking to the offender privately, pointing out that some are not getting the chance to share much and asking the offender's help in encouraging others.

(d) By privately telling the offender firmly but in love that they are dominating the group and preventing a full contribution from everyone. This can be accompanied by an explanation, again, of the group's purpose and method.

In groups where all share in turn and none interrupts (e.g. with Navigator material) some of these snags are avoided. Sometimes the group itself can light-heartedly deal with a dominater.

3. As pastor.

If argument begins (which would be more common in a discussion group but unusual in a sharing group) the leader should quietly help both sides to examine the points of the other with a view to understanding and learning from the other. If aggression is shown they should quietly ask why that point is difficult for the aggressive person to handle without strong feeling. When we stop to examine feelings they often dissolve. Where psychological, personality or other needs are evident, it may mean visiting the needy one personally and privately. Some people need to be in a therapeutic group or a Yokefellow Group (see Ch. 17) as well as, or in place of, a Bible sharing and Christian growth group. Ordinary pastoral needs however, ought to be met by the group's growing love and care for every member.

The three duties of the group leader are to ensure that the group's task is accomplished; to care for the individual members and to maintain the togetherness of the group. The leader also helps the group get on with its task of listening to God through Scripture and sharing honestly. The leader is sensitive to each member of the group and their needs. The leader helps the group to share and interact, to grow in love, in belonging, and in mutual care and accountability. It is a rich experience.

Other helpers.
Under the leader others may serve as host and hostess of the group (always a pair), as prayer leader, as pastoral care organiser, as time-keeper and anything else necessary.

After each meeting.
Following each meeting the leader should sit down and think it through.
Did the group get on with its task (listening to and talking about the Scripture passage)?
Did the group give everyone opportunity to share? Did any dominate? Were any left out?
Did the group have a sense of belonging together? Did it work well together?
Did any member show any need of personal attention or help?
Was there evidence of any particular potential or gift showing in any member that might be further looked for and finally trained and used?
What snags or difficulties need further thought and help?

The group leaders should meet together fairly often with the minister present (maybe as chairman) to share joys and encouragements, snags encountered that need to be discussed, help needed, potential seen in members, thoughts and insights on the material ahead and coherence of all groups in the one venture. They can then pray for all these things and for their own leadership.

How to prevent groups becoming turned inwards

In some churches there is a fear of small groups. Sometimes it is nothing more than a fear of change or of removing masks. Sometimes it comes from a wrong notion of the church which supposes that meetings which happen in church buildings are more sacred or more 'right' than those that take place in homes – a strange reversal of the New Testament. However, one main objection is that home groups can become gossip-shops or cliques – something which doesn't enrich the whole church but divides it. The danger is not unreal. How can it be avoided, and how, generally speaking can we prevent the groups from becoming turned inwards?

(a) The leader is the key to the group. If he is one who is totally committed to Jesus and the church (the Body of Jesus) the danger is removed. He must be one who has the gifts of a group leader (not there because he is a church official!) and appointed by the church. He must be simply but well trained. (*Lead Out*[42] by the Navigators is a simple but sufficient training manual.)

(b) At the first or second meeting of each group time should be given to agreeing and adopting pledges the group wish to make to each other for the good of the group. They need to consider things like confidentiality (this one is a must), regular attendance (except for serious reasons), punctuality, supporting each other in prayer, reading the same daily readings, pastoral care for one another in real love, total loyalty to Jesus and the local church, and so on. Once the pledges are agreed they should be printed on a card (perhaps with names, addresses and birthdays – not the year! – of every member), given to every member and read out in the first two or three meetings and occasionally thereafter. They should soon have become the way of the group's life.

All these things, especially the pledge to confidentiality will enhance group discipline and prevent the group giving in to the temptation to gossip.

(c) All new converts should be in a nurture group for the first year, preferably meeting weekly, ending with the discovery of gifts. Following that they can go into two groups, meeting alternate weeks – one a geographically placed group on the Watch and Pray pattern (see Ch. 10), and the other a group of people with the same gift which they exercise and improve together.

(d) Geographically based groups normally change over the year in our mobile society, or change by growth and division into two groups. But if such a group stays static it can change by the alteration of the neighbourhood boundaries for the groups at the end of each year.

(e) All groups should have the same general material or book for Bible study but freedom within that to use their own methods of study. So the groups have their own identity yet are consciously members of the family of groups.

(f) Each group meeting should have a time when they look outwards. Perhaps twenty minutes in each meeting could be given to a sharing of contacts, concerns and people they are praying for, followed by prayer for them. This time of looking outwards can be expanded if for two weeks in spring and two weeks in autumn the groups engage in outreach together, with simple training and preparation.

(g) The group can be pastorally responsible for its own members but can also extend this responsibility to others who live nearby and are not in groups; especially those housebound. This helps the outward perspective.

(h) When any group grows to twelve members it should split into two groups of six. Every group should understand from the beginning that this will be so, that it is something to aim at and celebrate when it happens. When this is imminent, prepare for it by splitting into two groups within the one home group for part of a meeting or two. (If groups are new or studying a specific book of the Bible new members should be asked to wait before joining so as not to disrupt the group.)

(i) The groups can meet together quarterly, this joint meeting taken by a different group in turn who talk about high points of their experience together and have a newstime for other groups to share briefly.

(j) Groups should feed relevant points and suggestions

to the church board, deacons or leaders who in turn can feed out relevant material to the groups for prayer and thought.

(k) If anything particularly helpful or exciting happens in or through a group, make a spot in the Sunday service when it may be shared.

(l) On occasion ask one of the groups to plan and conduct a Sunday evening service, using their own members appropriately and well.

(m) The group leaders should themselves meet once a month (early Sunday morning?) to share experiences, discuss difficulties or bring points for prayer. This gives the group leaders the experience of being in a group other than as leader and gives the sense of the church as a group of groups together. The minister may chair this meeting if he has the necessary skills. Otherwise appoint a good chairman/group leader and let the minister be present as a member.

All the points given above help prevent the church from falling into the trap of allowing its groups to become too inward-looking.

It has been said that there is nothing more difficult or more rich and satisfying than a good marriage. A good group is not so difficult if given the same understanding and care, but it is as joyful and enriching both to its members and to the whole church.

Note: For those who wish to set up groups and need further simple help and understanding, we recommend *How to Conduct Home Bible Classes* by Albert Wollen (Victor Books)[43].

Group exercises

1. Each take a large piece of paper and with coloured crayons or markers draw a series of pictures of the various groups you have been in (home, school, interests,

work, church etc.) Make the pictures and colours reflect your own feelings about each.

2. Share your pictures and each explain briefly what each one means.

3. What have you learned from this chapter about yourselves as a group? (you are, in studying this book, primarily a study or task group). In what ways can you improve as a group and what would you like to plan for the future when you have finished this book?

4. What have you learned that you might recommend to your church or put into practice in your church?

Chapter 16: Church Leadership and Witness

Leadership is one of the great words of our time. It is there whether we talk of commerce, politics or of sport. It is a key word in church life and in producing a witnessing church. Within this chapter we intend to broaden our scope to examine the characteristics of good church leadership (as opposed to group leadership).

It is, of course, possible for people to seek to become leaders from their own inner drives to achieve identity, significance or respect. This is a great temptation but it can be a paralysing factor in the life of the church or any organisation. It may prevent honesty and change because any suggested change will be heatedly opposed, not because it is wrong but because it challenges the pride and status of the leader and that has to be defended at all costs. Every leader needs to spend time with his Lord often, laying everything at His feet, totally at His disposal, and, above all, living moment by moment by grace and mercy alone. His identity and significance then come from God. He is a child of the King, beloved and redeemed at so great a price and called into royal service for others. His leadership he then holds in stewardship and obedience to the Saviour and is free to change, to take up work or to lay it down at the Master's will.

Characteristics of good church leadership

In a lively, witnessing church the leadership should constitute each of the following:

1. A corporate model for the church
What the leadership team is the whole church will increasingly tend to become.

We began our ministry with an incredible ignorance of the leadership of a church. Molly had been converted during the war and had changed her denomination. I had been converted just before the war, then did six years in the forces and a further six years in theological colleges. And that was in the days when colleges taught you all the academic subjects but very little about leading people. I remember conducting my first Church Meeting and doing quite happily until one member got up and said, 'Mr Chairman, you haven't put the substantive motion'. I had no idea what a substantive motion was in those days. I had to ask the speaker what it was. He told me, I put it and all was well!

But our first church was a Christian joy. It was full of loving, praying people and had ten men as a diaconate who were a real brotherhood of love and prayer. They taught me what ministry and leadership meant. We shared together, laughed together, prayed together and sometimes wept together. It was a small group dedicated to the service of Jesus and knit together by His Spirit. Needless to say the whole church reflected the same Spirit.

In another church I had a diaconate of sixteen people (by its number already outside the dynamics of the small group). Many of them were very important people in the town and found it hard not to be treated as important people, used to being listened to and getting their own way, on the diaconate. They were sixteen people of ability who never 'gelled' to make a spiritual leadership team. Consequently the church was a collection of 330 individuals who never gelled to make a church. Most of them were fine and lovely people but the body of Christ was spastic.

Johan Lukasse of the Belgian Evangelical Mission tells the story of church planting through his organisation.[44] They gather a team together and teach them for several months to live and share together, caring for each other, forgiving each other, praying for each other and learning each other's strengths, weaknesses and gifts. The team then goes out to plant a new church and is at the beginning the nucleus of the new church.

Lukasse puts great stress upon the training of the team. What that team becomes, he says, is the deciding factor in what the newly-planted church will become.

The leadership group is a model of what the church they serve is to be.

2. People of vision

One of the greatest needs of church leaders today is to escape from the ever-mounting pile of business and problems that means that all their time and effort is taken just to keep the routine wheels turning.

Our eyes should be fixed on Jesus, not on our problems. And a great deal of business should be cleared from our agendas completely and given to competent individuals or sub-groups to get on with. Everyone knows that if you ask a hundred people what colour you want the churchhall door painted, you will get a hundred answers and can waste endless time in debate without furthering the purposes of Jesus one jot. Such a matter should be given to someone with a knowledge of decorating and an eye for good colour while the church searches the Scriptures, prays and shares its insights and compulsions of the Spirit on mission.

We would recommend that alternate leaders' meetings be held in a home and that the full time be given to seeking God's visions and to prayer.

A forward-looking book can be of great help. Let each

221

leadership member read a chapter beforehand, perhaps several times, praying, asking God to reveal His meanings and purposes and meditating upon the trends and possibilities in the situation. The leaders then come to their vision-seeking meeting to share what God has given to them and to seek further together the mind and will of God. We would recommend a simple book like Peter Cotterell's *Church Alive*[45] for a beginning. Then, perhaps, Deitrich Bonhoeffer's *Life Together*[46] and, leading up to evangelism, Michael Green's *Evangelism – Now and Then*[47] or, of course, this book.

A positive thinking through of possibilities by a united team before God is exciting and the leadership is both changed and inspired by it.

3. People dedicated and growing

'Christian education' is constantly bedevilled in the church by its application to children and young people only. Immediately it becomes something to grow out of.

Christians who have stopped learning and growing into all that Jesus is and has for them are apt to become fossils. If the church is to be 'God's Pilgrim People' then its leadership must be ever growing both in depth and in width. To grow in depth alone is to become narrow and removed from life, reality and effectiveness. To grow in width alone is to become vague, wandering and increasingly silted up. The antidote to both is a total concentration on and dedication to Jesus in His Spirit and in all His purposes.

Douglas Hyde was a leading communist in the 1930's and became News Editor of the *Daily Worker*. After the Second World War, somewhat to his own surprise, he became a Christian. Writing of his conversion he tells of the great disappointment he felt in coming into the church only to find an almost total lack of the drive and passion that he had known in the communist movement and cells. In his book *Dedication and Leadership*[48] he writes:

222

'When I first went to work on the British Communist Party's daily paper, I was proud that I had been chosen for the work, proud to make whatever sacrifice was asked of me, but I was nonetheless conscious of the fact that I had willingly accepted a ludicrously small wage. I will admit that I felt slightly virtuous about this – until I met other members of the staff. Most of them were older than I was at that time, they had gone further in their careers (and some had gone very far indeed) and had had to make far higher sacrifices than I. Some of them were earning one tenth of what had been their salary when they had worked for the capitalist press. There were times when, small as our salaries were, these could not be paid at all.

Even when the paper became slightly more prosperous and the staff were technically given the union rate for the job, the sacrifice still continued. We got our pay packets, opened them and immediately gave eight-fourteenths of their contents to the Party and the paper.

Dedication perpetuates itself. It sets the tone and pace of the movement as a whole. If the majority of the members of an organisation are half-hearted and largely inactive, then it is not surprising if others who join it soon conform to the general pattern. If the organisation makes relatively few demands upon its members, and if they quite obviously feel under no obligation to give a very great deal to it, then those who join may be forgiven for supposing that this is the norm and that this is what membership entails.'

For all the evil of communism, there is much we have to learn from their dedication and drive. What they believe they believe absolutely, are willing to work hard for it and willing to sacrifice a great deal for it. Should we be or do less for Jesus?

4. Those who enable others to grow

The brief for church leaders is set out clearly in Ephesians 4 verses 11–12. It is there stated plainly that the ministry of the church is the daily and ordinary task of every church member. The job of the leadership is to equip the members for their ministry. 'The worst kind of leadership is that which is like a beech tree – magnificent to all outward appearance but nothing grows under it'.[49] The leader who does everything himself, however well he does it, is a bad leader. The leader who looks out for the potential in others and humbly helps them develop and use it is a good leader. Good leaders produce other good leaders all the time (2 Timothy 2: 2).

Too often the few do far too much and there is a collusion between leaders and led. The leaders want to do it all and the led are either willing to let them or they leave for more lively pastures. Too often jobs are either not handed over at all or are handed over suddenly, without training and often without accountability.

There ought to be no leader who is not constantly encouraging and equipping members to live a joyful, witnessing and total Christian life. And there ought to be no leader who is not associating someone else with himself in the work he is doing with a view to handing over the work in course of time. Delegation should normally be in three steps:

(a) You associate yourself with me and watch me do the work for a year.

(b) I will associate myself with you while you do the job and I am your helper for six months or a year.

(c) You do the job and I will be available for consultation if you want me.

Further, delegation must be, at the third stage *without interference* (however provoking it may be to see the new man adopting new ways) but with accountability to someone or somebody. Let's look at Douglas Hyde's outline of the communist method of building up recruits.[50]

'(a) Get the recruits to commit themselves publicly to the cause. (They usually began by selling the *Daily Worker* in the streets of their own neighbourhood.) The opposition and questions they got asked made them keen to learn answers and know more.

(b) Form small groups for study and sharing – life and action orientated. Teach recruits they are part of a world battle and that they are playing a significant part at a decisive time in it. Teach them that the world does not have to be the way it is. It can be changed. Teach them the force that can change it.

(c) Every person trained is to spread the news to others of his own kind, and to win respect for himself as a man.

(d) Those who are gifted are to be thoroughly trained for leadership.

(e) Everything is to be action orientated. Every lesson is to begin by our sharing what we did about last week's lesson and to end with asking what we are to do about this week's lesson.'

Have we a similar strategy to enable our new converts and members to grow as mature and active Christians? Or is it still true that the children of darkness are more shrewd than the children of light?

We need strong, competent leadership, not of the authoritarian kind but that which is devoted to Jesus and to the fulness of the people of Jesus and leads by its inherent quality and authentication.

5. *People who are listeners and encouragers*

Lawrence Crabb, in his excellent books on counselling,[51] says there are three levels of counselling;

(a) Loving encouragement. Ninety-five per cent of our church membership can give this to each other and certainly every leader should be giving to everyone all the time. As Crabb points out, many problems would never develop and would be contained and dealt with if loving and caring encouragement was general in the church.

(b) Low-level counselling of people with particular problems. Some church members have a gift for this and most leaders ought to be able to listen, to pray with people and to counsel at an easy level. It requires a pastoral heart, patience, a love for God and a love for people and a good knowledge of the Bible and its counsels.

(c) Deep counselling. This is for the highly gifted and the experts only. Few leaders would be able to do this but they ought to know which people or bodies they can refer others to when deep counselling is needed.

6. People who are selective

Jesus was highly selective. In order that the whole world might be blessed He confined Himself to one small nation. In order that all men everywhere should hear the gospel, He turned his back on the crowds that followed Him and selected twelve. Into those few He poured His whole heart, to them He gave most of His time and in them He invested His life and mission.[52]

Here is a right principle for leadership. It is always better to teach twelve deeply (that they may teach others) than to teach a hundred shallowly.

Our aim must always be for excellence – for quality not mere quantity.

One friend of ours whom we will call Eric found himself as the minister of a large, traditional and dull church. His early efforts to breathe life into it resulted in response only from a handful of people. He resolved therefore to keep the wheels turning for the rest but to give himself to the responding handful without stint. They formed themselves into a Bible study, sharing and witness group in which he found joy and the group grew in maturity and contagious blessing. Today, almost twenty years later, that church is lively and loving and its leaders are those who were in Eric's group.

At our last church in Chelmsley Wood we were led to an effective selectivity. Before we went there we had visited many new estates and discovered too many churches with over a hundred children and half-a-dozen adults totally unable to cope with so many children in traditional services. We were then forced to make it clear that as far as Sunday school was concerned we would take only the children whose parents attended church. We would tell the remaining children that a special meeting would be held for them on Wednesdays. Consequently on Sunday mornings we had a small group of children who were easy to cope with. And on Wednesday we had the whole premises and an adequate staff (who were not missing the Sunday service) to lead about eighty children who attended. It was selective and restrictive only that more might be blessed and a thorough work done.

Likewise we restricted each class to five children on the strict understanding that the teacher had not five children but five families to cultivate and work for. Once a class had five children others wanting to come were put on a waiting list. It increased regularity and keenness no end! The best work is selective.

7. People who are thorough

Not long ago we attended a meeting of Junior Christian Endeavour. The leader had done her job in appointing different children to play a part in the meeting but had not given them training. The appointed time to begin came and the girl who was to conduct the meeting went forward and announced the opening hymn. Immediately the leader interrupted to say, 'Oh, don't begin yet, Angela. I think there are one or two still to come'. Only half an hour later the leader asked the children to repeat the Christian Endeavour pledge including their pledge to punctuality! By agreeing to hold up the whole thing on behalf of the late children the leader had effectively taught them that their pledge really didn't matter. There could be no better preparation for a church life and a Christianity that does not matter than a leadership of this kind.

I remember with gratitude my own early Christian Endeavour training. Those taking part in a meeting were asked round to the house of the leader during the week previous, instructed and rehearsed. If I was doing a Scripture reading I had to read it out aloud three times every day during that week and another three times or more at the leader's house. I would be told to look at a person in the back row, pretend he was a little hard of hearing and to address myself plainly, clearly and audibly to him. Everything had to be done thoroughly and well because it was done for the Lord. Second best would not do ('Don't allow slackness to spoil your work' Rom.12: 11).

In my junior school (way back in the early 1930's) we had a boy called Charlie Lingwood. Charlie was mentally sub-normal and he had reached the age of ten without being able to read or write. Up to that time no teacher had bothered about that – Charlie was accepted as one who could not be expected to learn – and he simply sat quietly in every class and learnt nothing.

But when we were ten a new teacher came to the school. His name was Mr Collins. He was a good teacher and showed a personal interest in every boy. He spent time talking to Charlie and finding out his capacities. Then, with the parents' permission, he stayed an extra hour (totally unpaid) every day with Charlie using his own methods and with great patience drawing his limited abilities out into use. After eighteen months Charlie could read and within his limits could also write.

What Mr Collins taught me is that whether people's capacities are large or small, it is God's pleasure that they should be brought to their fulness and not neglected. That is the skill of leadership.

8. People with clear priorities

Once we understand that our Christian life and our daily living are the same thing, we are clear to make our priorities. Priority number one in Jesus is ministry to our partner and our family. Priority number two is our work and our working life which we are to make a love-offering to Jesus daily. Priority number three is what we do within church structures down at the church building.

If these three priorities had been observed in this order much heartbreak and stress in marriage and family life would have been avoided. (Leaders must set a clear example especially here as Paul points out in 1 Timothy 3.)

There are priorities too within the church structures and in the use of church money. Staff should come first, resources second and the buildings third. In Britain we usually reverse that!

In the matter of paid staff we need one extra for every 150 members. By that number the minister needs an assistant who will take a whole part of church life off his shoulders. It need not be another ordained person. It may indeed be someone gifted from the congregation. It will be someone who has a strength where the present minister or ministers are weakest. The need may be for a youth worker, an evangelism trainer and leader, an administrator, a counselling practitioner and trainer, a music and singing director, a Christian education leader or anything else.

Getting priorities right helps all the wheels run smoothly and is the job of leadership.

9, People willing to change

We have a great deal of sympathy with older people who find change difficult. There is so much change today that they look to find something that does not change. But we must not confuse eternal things with the means and forms by which they find expression. These must change or they simply become irrelevant. The Reformers did not dethrone the Pope to replace him with a fixed order of service or of church life but to proclaim Jesus Christ as Lord of all.

I remember listening to a long list of complaints about change from an older church member. 1910 had, he informed me, been the great age of Christianity, when the great preachers occupied the pulpits and 'there were extra seats in the aisles' because so many people came.

I sat in a comfortable chair and listened – and looked at his colour television, the wall-to-wall carpeting and his shining car outside the window! I would dearly have loved a magic wand to take him back to 1910 right then.

We must change and grow all the time as Christians. We must change and grow as a church. We must change and grow in leadership. One of the most difficult areas of change is that of church organisations. Sometimes leaders of organisations feel threatened and become highly defensive if church leaders speak of change. We believe that the leaders and helpers in every church organisation should, once a year, sit down togehter and, without any pressure from church leaders or anyone else, work honestly through such questions as:

(a) What are our aims?

(b) Are they truly New Testament aims?

(c) Are we achieving those aims?

(d) Are there simpler or more direct methods of achieving these aims?

(e) Are our aims and our work an integral part of the aims and work of the church or are we in danger of becoming something separate?

(f) Are we taking every opportunity of further developing our abilities and training?

(g) Are we thorough in our preparation and all we do?

(h) If we are dealing with children, are we cultivating and caring for their families too – putting the child in his proper context?

(i) Are we looking for hidden potential, encouraging and

developing it, bringing everyone to the fulness of his capacity whether that be large or small?

(j) Can we lay down everything in and about our organisation at Jesus' feet, utterly and unreservedly at His disposal?

10. People who share their faith

Not all church members have the gift of an evangelist. But all are called to witness. Leaders in the church, then, ought to be leaders in ordinary, low-key witness. If they are not they quench and dull the work of the Holy Spirit and the evangelical zeal of God's people.

Each church court or diaconate should send every one of its new members to a Teach and Reach (Evangelism Explosion) clinic or, if the church is in an urban area, to the extended and excellent course run by the Ichthus Fellowship in London.[53] Thereafter they should spend one day in retreat every year, preparing for it by all having read the same related book beforehand, and having full discussion sessions on the immediately relevant chapters or themes.

One deep need of the churches today is to escape from the idea that church leadership constitutes dealing with business or administrative problems and to return to the priority of pastoral care, equipping, leadership by example and vision giving.

11. People who teach by what they are

We are sometimes asked what is the best kind of youth organisation for today. Our answer is always the same: the name or kind of organisation is not half so important as the person of the leader.

If the leader is a deep and warm Christian, an encouraging and inspiring personality, one who can speak of Jesus enthusiastically and naturally, youth will come and they will become keen Christians.

I well remember the last Sunday school class I was in. I was thirteen, and one of a group of eight lively and unruly boys. The class leader was a dear old man named Mr Crane. Each Saturday he would have one of us up to his home, and usually took us out for a walk, followed by a cream tea, during which he got to know us. He cared deeply about us and he prayed regularly for us.

I remember that we often played him up in class. None of us were committed as Christians and I am sorry that Mr Crane did not live long enough to see my conversion. I would have loved to have said, 'Mr Crane, all your work and prayer with that unruly mob was not in vain. Some of us are now people of Jesus'.

Mr Crane was truly a man of God. To this day I cannot remember a single word he ever said to us – although I am sure he was a good teacher and prepared well – but I shall never forget what that man was. That taught me more than any words and that went deep. It remains warmly in my heart and mind to this day.

Church leaders should be good friends, counsellors and teachers. But most important of all is what they are. That will teach more deeply and permanently then anything else. A church leader should have many gifts. But what matters most is that he is a man of God.

Motivating and enlisting helpers

Do's and don'ts

Don't ask for volunteers.

Don't just look around for people who can be pressed into 'doing something for the church'.

Don't appoint only those you like or who will agree with your opinions.

Don't depend on vague knowledge of the personalities of people you are asking to become involved.

Don't assume people know what the job is and what its possibilities are.

Don't assume people know how to do the job.

Don't leave people to get on with the job alone.
Don't criticise or show lack of interest.
Don't let the few do too much.

On the other hand:
Do use talent-search cards for every member.
Do have an individual or group within the church
who can take charge of 'personnel' matters.
Do pray and think carefully before appointing
people.
Do personally invite those whom God indicates.
Do provide a clear job description in writing.
Do give opportunity for preliminary experience by
allowing the person being considered a period as
apprentice and by giving simple but thorough
training.
Do have a system of accountability.
Do encourage, recognise and praise achievement
constantly.
Do keep all eyes open for potential in others that can
be discovered, developed and deployed.

Conclusion

A leader in commerce is the boss; he is qualified by
competing with others and beating them, his power
comes from the hierarchical structure, his purpose is to
better himself, his success is evaluated on the basis of
quantity. 'Those who are rulers in the ungodly world
lord it over them . . . But it shall not be so among you'
(Mark 10: 42–45).

A leader in the work of Jesus is a servant of the Lord,
recognised by God's people; he is qualified to lead by
his standing as a man of God, by his gifts and by his
ability to lead others in the Spirit of Jesus. His authority
is a moral one and his work is evaluated on the basis of
quality.

Consider the list of leadership qualities given in 1 Timothy 3: 8–13.[54]

1. '*Serious . . .*' Not light or frivolous but in earnest. (No implication of lack of a good sense of humour.)

2. '*Not double-tongued . . .*' Utterly trustworthy and lovingly truthful.

3. '*Not addicted to much wine . . .*' Not self-indulgent but temperate and self-disciplined.

4. '*Not greedy for gain . . .*' Not having a selfish, acquisitive or money-centred mind.

5. '*Holding the mystery of the faith with a clear conscience . . .*' Mature in the Christian faith and in living it out in practice.

6. '*Let them be tested first . . .*' Those who have already proved themselves in Christian life and leadership.

7. '*Having wives [who are] serious, no slanderers, temperate, faithful . . .*' Possessing wives who share their devotion to Jesus; not gossips but women of discretion and self-control who can be trusted.

8. '*Husband of one wife . . .*' Not a polygamist or a philanderer. A faithful, loving husband.

9. '*Managing their children . . .*' Building deep, sound and true relationships in family life in which children grow in love to their fulness in body, mind and spirit.

10. '*Managing well their households . . .*' Showing loving Christian leadership in family devotions and in all home and family affairs and connections.

Group exercises

1. Each make a list of the top five qualities or requirements needed in a church leader today. As each list is read put the qualities on to a wall sheet (many will overlap and will not need to be put up twice). Now agree together on a 'top ten'. Make the list known to others.

2. Each share what have been the greatest helps and the

greatest hindrances in your own experience of leadership (either as a leader yourself or in observing others).

3. You have a young man in your congregation with leadership potential although he has only recently been converted. He says God has called him to the Christian ministry although he has never yet preached or led in Christian work. What would you say to him? What tests would you apply? What training and help would you give to him?

4. Here are some leadership styles:
(a) Authoritarian. One man rules.
(b) Paternalistic. One man leads and guides.
(c) Democratic. What the majority says goes.
(d) Permissive. Anyone can do anything.
(e) Traditional. We do what has always been done and fill the roles expected of us.

What is wrong with these styles? What principles and style of leadership do we really need in a Christian church?

Chapter 17: The Place of Prayer

In this age of new challanges and ventures we are in danger of forgetting that these are the fruit of a new and lively spirit, not the heart of it. We are indeed called to challenge, action and to new structures. But there is a call prior to that. We are called first to a total commitment to Jesus Christ as both Saviour and Lord, and to keep our lives warm at the hearth of His life. The first thing God wants is not our action but that He should fill us with the Spirit of Jesus.

How do we win people for the Lord unless we first love them? And how do we love them unless first we receive that love as a gift from God? And how do we receive that gift from God unless we pray?

What is prayer?

Prayer is fellowship with our heavenly Father. It is having the windows of the soul ever-open to Him. It is talking to Him about everything – thanking Him, saying sorry, asking for His help and guidance, telling Him we love Him and bringing every part and detail of life to Him to know His meaning and purpose in it and to receive the touch of His Spirit upon it. I like the mnemonic that prayer is:

P raising God
R epentance
A sking God for things for ourselves and others
Y ielding ourselves to Him in everything.

I like the definition of prayer as 'opening the door in any situation to let Jesus in'. Tough situations are transformed when He comes in. I like the definition of prayer as 'the upturned face of a little child bringing some broken thing to the Father to be mended'. Broken lives, broken hearts, broken homes and broken relationships have all been mended by the pierced hands of the Carpenter.

I also like the definition of prayer as our Daily Routine Orders. In the forces during the war first thing every morning we had to receive the Daily Routine Orders – a note of events and responsibilities for the day. We need to be reminded that prayer is not just asking God for things. Even less is it telling God what we want. It is fundamentally the giving of our lives, circumstances and concerns to Him for all that He wants – letting Him fill us with His Spirit and purpose; letting Him be Lord.

What happens when people pray

There are a number of churches throughout Britain who are experiencing great blessing today. They are of many different kinds and are in every area of the land. There are some in the inner city, some in rural areas, some in council housing estates – some in every type of situation. No longer is it possible to say 'It can't be done here'. When we meet such a church we always try to find out where the blessing began and we are told so often that it began with a prayer group.

In Somerset a small group of young married women became concerned for their non-Christian husbands. They began to meet together to pray. Early in their prayer fellowship the Lord said to them, 'Don't nag your husbands. Don't push them to become Christians or try to get them to come to church. That will only send them further away. You are to be living demonstrations of the love of Jesus to them and lift them up to Him in loving prayer'. Within a year all but one of the husbands were new-born Christians.

The fact is that, as the Yokefellow Groups[55] teach, we cannot change other people despite all our anxious trying and fretting. We can only let Jesus change us, until our lives become a channel of His love and grace toward others.

In Dumfries there is a church that was once down to twelve members. One of the members there said, 'We cast ourselves entirely upon God. We put Him first. We were steadfast in prayer. It began slowly but the intercessors increased and we began to feel and see the blessing of God'. Today that church is not only lively but is giving new life to other churches nearby.

It is notable how many churches now experiencing new life and energy began by being brought low – literally brought to their knees.

'If you, being evil, know how to give good gifts to your children, how much more shall your heavenly Father give the Holy Spirit to them that ask Him' (Luke 11: 13).

Prayer in the New Testament

We have the following New Testatment examples of how to pray.

1. The example of Jesus
It is impossible to read the gospel story without being impressed with Jesus as a man of prayer. There is no turning point in His life in which we do not find Him praying. At His baptism He was praying (Luke 3: 21); before choosing the Twelve He spent a night communing with His Father (Luke 6: 12); at Caesarea Philippi (Luke 9: 18), in the garden of Gethsemane He prayed in great agony (Luke 22: 41–44) and He even died praying: 'Jesus cried out with a loud voice "Father into Your hands do

I commend my spirit" and when He had said this He died' (Luke 23: 46).

It was not only the crisis points that found Jesus praying. Prayer was the normal atmosphere of His everyday living. His was a constant practice of the presence of God. He rose early in the morning to pray (Mark 1: 35), He ended a day of pressure and toil in prayer (Mark 6: 46) and on so many occasions His heart and thoughts flew heavenward (Mark 7: 34, John 12: 28).

Prayer was as natural to Jesus as breathing and He bids us to pray and to live in constant fellowship with God too (Luke 11: 1–13, 18: 1–14, Matt. 26: 41)

2. The example given in Acts

The New Testament Church was full of prayer. Remember that great occasion when Peter and John were going to the Temple to pray. There they met the crippled man who asked them for money (as the schoolboy wrote 'he had lost the use of both his legs so he sat and asked for arms') and gave him not money but healing in the Name of Jesus (Acts 3). The man was jumping and leaping and praising God but the Temple authorities were not very pleased about it. They arrested Peter and John and brought them before the council in Jerusalem. There was not a lot the council could do because so many people knew that a miracle had taken place but they were determined 'to stop this thing from spreading'. They therefore threatened Peter and John that if they spoke publicly about Jesus again they would be in for real trouble. They then let them go. Peter and John went straight back to the other disciples and they had a prayer meeting. 'Sovereign Lord God of heaven and earth and sea,' (they had no doubt about who was in authority – and it was not the council in Jerusalem!) 'Give us boldness to speak your word' (Acts 4: 24 and 29) – the very thing they had been ordered not to do. And when they prayed the whole place in which they were meeting was shaken, they were all filled with the Holy Spirit and they spoke boldly for Jesus.

That story has a modern counterpart. Duncan Campbell, speaking of the very remarkable spiritual awakening in Lewis, in the Outer Hebrides, during the early 1950's, tells how he went to Lewis 'on an urgent request from praying people'. In one village they met with great opposition and were driven to spend a night in prayer. It was an extraordinary prayer meeting and Campbell (a dour Scot and abhorrent of exaggeration) records that 'the house shook like a leaf, the dishes rattled on the sideboard' and they walked out 'to find the whole community alive with an awareness of God'.[56]

At another time Paul and Silas were in Philippi and because of their preaching they were arrested, severely flogged and thrown into prison. They were put into the inner cells with their feet fastened in the stocks (Acts 16: 12-34). How would you feel if you were in a filthy prison, your back in agony and running blood and your feet fast in the stocks? At midnight Paul and Silas prayed and sang praises to God. What on earth can you do with men like that? You beat them, push them into a dungeon and fasten them up and all they do is pray and praise! Is it any wonder that the very jailer was converted?

These men did not care whether they were flogged or applauded; whether they were in a dungeon or a palace. The vital sense of the presence of Jesus with them and their habit of bringing all things to Him and praising Him in all circumstances held their hearts and minds.

This was the spirit of that early Church and the reason why it turned the world upside down in its time.

3. The example of the Epistles
The Epistles, like their writers, are full of prayer and encouragement to pray:
'Don't worry over anything whatever. Tell God every detail of your needs in earnest and thankful prayer' (Phil 4: 6 JBP).

'Pray without ceasing' (1 Thess 5: 12)

'If any among you is troubled, let him pray. If anyone is doing well let him praise the Lord' (James 5: 13)

'I will therefore that men pray everywhere from the heart, without resentment in their minds and without doubting' (1 Tim 2: 8).

And, above all, that glorious chapter of Romans 8 in which Paul says the Holy Spirit gives us that tremendous knowledge that we are the children of God, living moment by moment as children of the King by grace alone. He tells us how it is the Holy Spirit who helps us to pray. He inspires us to pray, He helps our weakness in prayer and when our words fail He intercedes for us. Whether Paul is referring here to those times when we are overcome by a sense of our own mortality and sin, or to those times when our longings and feelings are too deep for words does not matter. At all these times when we do not know how to frame our prayers, God's Spirit within us prays for us. 'And God who knows the heart's secrets understands the Spirit's intention as He prays for those who long for God's will'.

It is no wonder that this chapter ends with a great promise and a shout of Christian triumph and praise (Romans 8: 38, 39).

The importance of prayer

Let us look briefly at some of the points and promises about prayer that relate to witness.

1. Prayer together

God has given special promises to those who pray together (Matthew 18: 19,20). This means more than just praying in the same place at the same time. It implies a deep togetherness in the bonds of Christ and in His purpose. It is quite possible for a congregation all to sit through a prayer in church (or even a time of open prayer) and *yet never to have prayed together*. People who pray together are those between whom the barriers are down, who love one another in the love of Jesus and know themselves bound to Him and to each other in His blood bonds. The blessing which is coming today from so many prayer groups and Prayer Triplets[57] is that they have learned to take off their masks, to love one another, to forgive one another, to minister to one another even as Jesus loves, forgives and ministers to them. Even apart they pray together as well as pray for each other.

Many of our prayer meetings in time past have weakened and died because we met but did not meet; we said and listened to prayers but we did not pray together.

2. *All at God's disposal*

The keynote of Christian prayer is not telling God what we want but placing our whole lives – our home, work relationships, habits and will – together with specific situations, completely at God's disposal. We ask Him what He wants and open our hearts to the purpose and Spirit of Jesus. 'You don't get what you need because you don't ask God for it. And when you do ask He does not give to you, because you ask in the wrong spirit – you only want to satisfy your own desires' (James 4: 3).

We soon discover that before God wants us to do anything, He wants us to become something. He wants us first to surrender our own way and will and to receive the Spirit of Jesus who will fill us with new desires (those of Jesus Himself) and will enthrone Jesus as Lord in our lives and circumstances. God is not an emergency hospital or the storeman who is to be persuaded to supply our wants. He is the Lord. Beside Him there is none else. He alone is God. He always was. He always will be.

3. *Specific prayer*

True prayer is spreading before God the present and particular circumstances, just as Hezekiah spread before the Lord the threatening letter from the Assyrians (2 Kings 19: 14). It is not enough to pray vaguely or generally 'God bless my neighbours'. Pray for specific neighbours, friends or relatives and for specific situations and needs.

Let us use a sanctified imagination in praying for people; enter lovingly into their circumstances and feelings, 'stand in their shoes' and then lift them up and place them in the pierced hands of Jesus for His touch and for His ministry. Let us also listen for what God wants us to be and do and to seek to understand God's meaning and purpose for us in this place.

If you have not already done so, we would ask you now to do two things. First take pen and paper and put down the names of everyone God has put it into your heart to pray for. This is to be part of your prayer list. If it is long divide it into seven so that you spend time in prayer for every person named at least once a week. Do have a specific list of people you are praying for.

Second, ask God if He will give you two other people with whom you can meet as a Prayer Triplet. The three of you can meet at any time and any place convenient to you, but meet regularly and pray for specific people. Prayer Triplets normally pray for nine people – three for each person in the Triplet. Some of God's greatest blessings have come through prayer triplets – don't miss such a blessing.[58]

4. Positive prayer
We remember one church man who suffered from a nervous breakdown. He came to us for help and especially to ask why God did not answer his prayers for healing. We asked how he prayed and discovered that his prayers were a 'battering at the gates of heaven' in which he worked himself up into a highly frenzied and nervous state. His prayers were in fact a rehearsal of his unbelief.

Our advice was that he adopted a very different way

of prayer, and we told him that God was indeed answering and what He was saying was, 'Yes. I will to heal you. Now just shut up babbling and working yourself into a worse state and relax and let my healing enter your life'. We suggested he first read a story of Jesus healing in the gospels. Then he should spend his prayer time horizontal on the floor, first consciously relaxing every muscle in his body, beginning with his feet and going right up to his head and at the same time quietly picture in his mind the scene and the story of Jesus he had read. Having let his imagination reconstruct and feel the incident, he should then see himself as the one whom Jesus healed and receive His healing into heart, mind and body. That man began a steady recovery from that time.

Too much prayer is negative. We rehearse our resentments, our frustrations, our hatreds, our impatience or our fears and they become worse as a result.

There are ministers whose maxim seems to be, 'Where grace abounds, sin shall much more abound'. They preach on sin and sinfulness almost exclusively and their prayers major on sin and wallow in our wretched state as sinners. People come out from such a service depressed, bedraggled and demeaned.

Thank God there are many more who do not ignore the fact of sin but who major on the wonder of God's redeeming work in Christ and in the miracle of grace. People come out from their services filled with reverence and love for Jesus and a great joy in belonging to Him and an enthusiasm to tell others of Him.

The depressed are not likely to be good or attractive witnesses for Jesus. Those who can never stop thanking God for His mercy in Jesus are. In prayer let us maintain the positive approach.

If we are concerned about a besetting sin let us not concentrate on that but on its opposite in Jesus. If we are praying for a non-Christian partner or a difficult neighbour let us not nag at God about them or turn over our resentment in our prayer but pray that they may be filled with God's love and blessing and that Jesus will keep us free in His goodness and grace to be a channel of His love and blessing to them. Positive prayer changes us as well as others and leaves us as Spirit-filled and joy-filled witnesses who believe that God can do great and glorious things.

5. *The prayer of praise*

Praise has brought new life to worship and to prayer today. It has lifted our eyes and minds off the domination of problems and problem-solving on to Jesus, His glory, His grace and His purpose. It has lifted our prayers from plaintive pleading to joyful believing.

I do not believe that God sends evil or ever wills evil but I do believe that God in the very worst of situations can bring good out of evil and that we should pray with praise that this is so.

As Joseph said to his brothers about their cruel treatment of him, 'You meant it to me for evil but God meant it to me for good' (Genesis 50: 20).

'God works all things together for good to those who love Him' (Romans 8: 28). Do you believe that? Then thank Him for it.

Praise coming out of the heart is the sign that the King is in residence there. In His presence is the fulness of joy.

6. *Prayer in Jesus' Name*

There are many hindrances to prayer mentioned in the New Testament: disobedience to Jesus (John 15: 6), unforgiveness of others (Mark 11: 25, Matthew 5: 43–46 and 6: 14–15), lack of faith (James 1: 6–8), unconfessed sin (I John 1: 6–9 and Psalm 66: 18), self-pride (Luke 18: 9–14) and so on.

One important phrase in prayer guides us away from such hindrances. It is 'In the Name of Jesus' (John 15: 16). This is not a signing-off phrase or a magic formula.

It means that we submit our prayer through Jesus and in character with all He is and all He purposes. As the schoolboy wrote, 'It means we can ask of God anything that Jesus would sign His Name to'! This is both a censor to our prayers and a challenge to the spirit in which we pray. Is our aim that which pleases us or that which pleases Jesus and glorifies God?

Conclusion

The gas man cometh.

One morning we awoke to find our front room full of gas. We rang the gas company to tell them their gas was escaping and an hour later a gas fitter rang our door bell. He asked for a cup of water and some detergent and we obliged. He put the detergent into the water and stirred it around with his finger and then rubbed the solution over the gas pipe. A bubble came up near a joint. 'There's your leak', he said, 'It needs that nut tightened. I'll do it in a jiffy'. We asked him whether he would like tea or coffee and went to put the kettle on.

Twenty minutes passed and he had still not appeared so we went in to see how he was getting on. He had finished the job and was standing in front of our book shelves looking at all the books.

'Do you like books?' we asked.

'Yes,' he said, 'especially Christian ones'.

'Are you a Christian?' we enquired.

'Yes,' he answered. 'I've been one now for over a year'.

We took him for his cup of coffee and asked how he became a Christian.

It began, he said, when he married a girl whose mother was a Christian. His mother-in-law witnessed to him about Jesus and kept on until he got fed up with it and told her bluntly to stop it. She did, wise woman, but she and her daughter (also a Christian by this time) prayed for him.

A short time later he had to go into hospital with internal pains the doctors could not diagnose. He was 'under observation' but three days later he suddenly felt the pains go and a great fitness and well-being come upon him.

That afternoon his wife and her mother came to visit and asked how he was. 'I'm well,' he said, 'I've never felt fitter in all my life'.

'When did that happen?' they asked.

'Just after half past twelve,' he answered. 'It was like a miracle.'

'Well,' said the mother, 'we had a special prayer group for you today from twelve until one o'clock.'

Suddenly God was blazingly real to our gas man and he committed his life to Jesus Christ soon afterwards. Where there is love and prayer miracles happen. Only God can make people new. But God needs channels through whom he can work. The channels are those people who have learned to love and to pray. That is our part.

Lord, teach us to love that we stay always open to others. Lord, teach us to pray that we stay open to You.

Group exercises

1. Let each member of the group share what has come home to them most strongly personally through this book.

2. Let each member of the group say what they feel is most important for your church arising from study of this book. Agree on a short statement to be sent to the leaders of the church with suggestions arising from your study and thought.

3. Each take a newspaper and find:
(a) a headline or sentence that you would like to give a Christian comment on;
(b) an advertisement or sentence that makes you think of someone you would like to pray for.
Each in turn share first (a), then (b).

4. Pray for others you have mentioned. Pray for each other.

Postscript by Lewis

During the Second World War, I was for some time a member of the RAF night fighter squadron which patrolled the English Channel each night. Up there at 30,000 feet, with everything blacked out below, we often felt much more like riders of the universe rather than creatures of planet earth. Down here the world constantly presses in upon us and it is sometimes difficult to believe in God. Up there it was sometimes difficult to believe in the world but God filled the whole vast universe.

My favourite was the dawn patrol. We would see dawn break from up above and then return to base only to see it happen all over again at earth level.

But the impressive thing was the coming of dawn seen from way above the earth. In the deep darkness there would first appear a small green glow on the eastern horizon. It would begin to grow and from it green fingers of light would begin to reach out into the sky. Then where the small green glow first appeared would come a touch of gold and from it fingers of gold would begin to reach out and claim the sky. And then the sun would rise. A new day had begun.

When we look around in our land today we see both darkness and opposition and the promise of a new dawn. Green fingers are already reaching out – people seeking for meaning and for God, new life and love in so many churches, new joy in worship, home groups growing everywhere and a new openness to God and to each other.

And there are the fingers of gold too – a new confidence and trust in Jesus, a new obedience to the Word of God, a new sense of the Spirit of Jesus among us making all things new with His creative life and love.

We believe a new day of God is about to burst upon us. Brothers and sisters, look up and pray for our land.

Appendix 1: The Witness Simulation Game

Outline

Taking 1½ hrs		Taking 2½ hrs
5 mins	Opening prayer or devotion	10 mins
5 mins	General explanation. Form into groups A and B.	10 mins
5 mins	Read explanation to groups	5 mins
5 mins	Time to consider	10 mins
15 mins	Visitation A to B	15 mins
5 mins	Re-group. Change rooms and roles. Read explanation to groups.	10 mins
5 mins	Time to consider	10 mins
15 mins	Visitation B to A	15 mins
20 mins	Re-assemble. Form into sixes. Consider what you have learned using Question Sheet.	30 mins
10 mins	Reporting	25 mins
5 mins	Brief prayer	5 mins

Introduction for Leaders (see also above outline)

The Witness Simulation Game is an excellent introduction to a conference or a series of sessions on personal witness for Christ. It 'breaks the ice', raises an awareness of the need for help and instruction and enables the leader to know where the people are and begin there.

To play the Game you will need:

Two leaders and a helper.

Two rooms – one sufficiently large to accomodate the main activities.

Enough chairs for everyone – some at least must be easily moveable!

Material reproduced from this appendix: ideally everyone should have a copy of this book, but otherwise the respective sheets can be photocopied or retyped without any infringement of copyright. Sufficient role sheets are needed, together with a question sheet for everyone to be used at the end of the game. The leaders should also obviously have a copy of the instructions for each group.

Overhead projector or large sheet of paper which can be pinned up at end of game to summarize group's findings.

The Game can last either one-and-a-half or two-and-a-half hours: use whichever timescale on the outline above suits you best. This includes short opening devotions and closing prayer. The helper or one of the leaders is time-keeper throughout and must keep time strictly.

After the opening devotions, one leader explains briefly to all that they are going to play a Simulation Game and that half the group will act the role of visitors in an evangelistic visitation campaign from the local church. The other half will be visited, and will play out certain written roles which will be given to them.

The people are then divided into two equal groups: Group A are the visitors and Group B those being visited (if there is an odd number the helper can join in to make an equal division possible). Group B must go into the room with enough chairs for all. Group A go into another room. One leader goes with each group and the helper with Group B.

The leader of Group A reads the written instructions (see p. 256) to his group. They then subdivide into small groups (of three) and are given about ten minutes to think together about what they will say and do while visiting. The leader of Group B, meanwhile reads the written instructions (see p. 257) to his Group. Group B subdivides into small groups and role papers are distributed (unless, of course, everyone has a copy of *Love Won Another*). Use three of the roles given in this appendix and share them out amongst the small groups. They then have about ten minutes to consider together how they will play their role.

The chairs should now be completely rearranged into pairs. Group A then enter, visit Group B on a one-to-one basis, carrying out an evangelistic 'visit'. After about fifteen minutes the visitation is stopped, and the groups swap over and divide again into their separate rooms. The exercise is then repeated, using the three remaining roles (or think up your own).

Finally, when this second 'visitation' is completed the groups rejoin together, and divide again into roughly groups of six in order to disccuss what has been learnt, using the questions on the Question Sheet (see p. 263). This lasts for thirty minutes. One leader then takes charge and, question by question, asks each group to report. The answers in brief form should be put on an overhead projector or written on a very large piece of paper on the wall. Close with a brief prayer.

Instructions to 'visiting' Group

1. We are going to pretend that your church has organised an Evangelistic Campaign, and that you are the visitors.

2. In ten minutes' time you are going out to share your faith with someone else.

3. As it is not a real visit, you won't have to go into the street and knock on doors. You will go into the room where the others are, pick one of them, sit beside them and do an evangelistic visit just as you would in reality.

4. The others have been told that you are coming and have been told what kind of people they are to pretend to be. One or two have to pretend to be hostile to the Church. If you get one of these, don't worry or take it personally – it's just a game.

5. You will have twenty minutes to get to know them, befriend them, and share your faith if you can.

6. Remember two things:

(a) you go with God in your heart, and (b) it's only a game, so relax and don't worry. Enjoy it!

7. First we are going to pretend we are in the Church Hall and we are going visiting in ten minutes. Just turn your chairs so that you are in groups of three and spend the time thinking about what you will do and say, talking about it and praying.

Instructions to 'visited' Group

1. We are going to pretend we are just ordinary non-Christian people living in the neighbourhood.
2. In ten minutes' time the local church is going to send some of its members to visit us on an evangelistic campaign.
3. Now please move the chairs to form into small groups of about three.
4. In a moment you will receive instructions telling you what kind of person you are to be when your visitor comes. You will have ten minutes to read, think and talk about your roles, and to get yourself ready to be that kind of person when your visitor arrives.
5. When the visitors arrive everyone must move again so that they have a vacant chair beside them, put their hand up high and keep it up until they have a visitor with them. They will visit one-to-one.
6. Keep details of your roles secret. Do not mention them or show them to anyone.

Leaders then give out role sheets – the same role to each group of three. On the first 'visitation' give out the first three role sheets ('Indifferent', 'Hostile', 'Shy'). When the visiting is later reversed give out the last three ('Guilty', 'Lonely', 'Hindu'). Others can, of course be written and added to better match the needs of your own area.

When the discussion is over and visitors arrive the leader should remind Group B of instruction 5.

Group B roles

The indifferent person

In a few minutes someone is going to attempt to share their faith with you. You begin as one quite indifferent to spiritual things.

1. If they begin by talking about spiritual things, you will not smile or encourage them. Tell them you are not bothered about things like that.

2. If they begin by showing you personal friendship or love, you will respond by smiling and taking an interest in them personally.

3. You have a partner who is difficult to live with and you have a daughter in hospital. You will not mention these unless you are asked about them.

4. You will not talk about spiritual things until, and unless, the other person has first shown an interest in your partner or your daughter and listened to you with love and concern as you talked.

5. The word 'church' turns you off completely. If the other person really cares about you, you are willing to talk or listen about Jesus Christ, but not about the church.

6. If the other person really shows love and care to you and wins you as a person, you will listen to their message and be really interested in anything they have to say about Jesus Christ.

7. Keep these instructions secret. Don't mention or show them to anyone.

The hostile person

In a few minutes someone is going to attempt to share their faith with you. You begin as one hostile to spiritual things.

1. If they begin by talking about spiritual things, tell them you are hostile. You once had a neighbour who was a 'leading light' in their church but was a very bad

neighbour to you. Tell them the story forcefully and at length about his or her bad ways.

2. If they respond by showing you personal friendship and love, you will begin to take an interest in them personally, if they listen to you with concern, you will be prepared to listen to them.

3. You have a daughter whose marriage is in the process of breaking up. You are deeply worried about it but will not mention it unless the other shows a real and loving interest in you and in your family.

4. If the other person has really listened to you, and shown concern for you and your family, you will be prepared to listen to them as they share their faith in Christ.

5. If their sharing is only to invite you to go to their church, you will clam up and be hostile. If they talk about Jesus Christ, you will be interested.

6. Keep these instructions secret. Don't mention or show them to anyone.

The shy person

1. In a few minutes someone is going to attempt to share their faith with you.

2. You are a very shy person with a great inferiority complex which you do everything to cover up.

3. As a child you went to the very church the other person comes from, but you don't want to reveal that in case they try and get you back. At the age of fourteen you 'made a decision for Christ' and had a great time of spiritual blessing for a year before you were led away by non-Christian friends. You are not willing to reveal that either.

4. If the other person just wants you to come to church, you will not be interested.

5. If the other person shows you real love and concern, you will be ready to listen to them. Deep down you long to return to Christ but feel that you are not worthy and couldn't be a real Christian anyway. If the other person

is loving and caring enough you might get around to admitting it.

6. If you do get around to honest talking about spiritual things, ask the other what you have to do to become a Christian again.

Keep these instructions secret. Don't mention or show them to anyone else.

The guilty person

1. In a few minutes someone is going to attempt to share their faith with you.

2. You are married, with one child who was conceived before marriage. You feel very wrong about that although you would not admit the fact or your feeling to anyone unless they had come quite close to you in real love and concern.

3. Your relations with your partner are a bit strained too. He or she is not very loving and you long for a loving, warm relationship with him or her. She or he is also quite anti-religion and if you became a Christian it might cause more trouble.

4. If the person talking to you simply wants you to come to church, you will be totally disinterested. If they speak about Jesus Christ and forgiveness you will be interested although perhaps slow to admit it at first.

5. If you do get around to honest talking about spiritual things ask the other person to tell you clearly what you have to do to be a Christian.

The lonely person

1. In a few minutes someone is going to attempt to share their faith with you.

2. You are very lonely and delighted to have them talk to you.

3. You are also determined not to appear lonely and would never admit it unless the other person showed

such love and concern for you personally that you felt they really cared.

4. You don't know much about Jesus and don't care much unless they speak about Him as a friend and a living presence.

5. If the visitor simply wants you to come to church you will resist that. They are all snobs anyway and you don't want to go. You think churches ought to stop all these funny services and run bingo and whist drives to get people together.

6. You desperately need friends and will respond to personal friendship and to the concept of the friendship of Christ. The rest is a non-starter although you will keep the other person talking just for company.

7. If you do get around to honest talking about spiritual things, ask the other person to tell you clearly what you have to do to be a Christian.

The hindu person

1. In a few minutes someone is going to attempt to share their faith with you. You are an immigrant, very polite but a hindu.

2. You, your extended family and your people in India have a very deep faith in many gods and goddesses. You all pray three times a day.

3. You have been in England for two years and are shocked at 'Christians' (all English people are Christians to you). They are racially prejudiced, greedy and materialistic.

4. You are quite happy to agree with all they say about Jesus Christ. He is one of many gods and prophets and you are quite prepared to worship Him – and all the others too.

5. You like to talk about Jesus but you are totally unin- terested in any attempts to get you to go to their church. You have your own temple and your own people who are much more devout and spiritual than 'Christians'.

6. You believe in re-incarnation and like to discuss it.

7. You have two sons of teenage who are becoming materialistic and unruly, like the English people, and you are very worried about them.

Question sheet

For use in de-briefing pairs, now in groups of six. Each member is to answer every question in turn.

1. What is the main thing that you have learned through this whole exercise?

2. What are the greatest difficulties in your sharing of the faith with others?*

3. What turns you off some of the people who have tried to share their faith with you?

4. What are the most important points to learn if we want to share our faith with others?

5. What would you want to include in a simple training course in sharing the faith?

* When replies are reported it is interesting to see how many of the difficulties are within ourselves.

Appendix 2: The Survey Form

Hints on use

1. Never use a survey form unless you honestly want the information you are collecting.

2. It is better to go singly (perhaps one on each side of a street) but if you really feel in need of psychological support then go in twos. Take a clipboard, plenty of forms and two pens.

3. Write down the answers people give in their own words. If someone gives a very long answer then you will have to summarise it (in one phrase or sentence if possible) but try to do so using their words, not yours. Also add, perhaps at the bottom of the form, any significant phrases they say (e.g. 'No-one from a church has ever called on me').

4. When the door opens say, 'I am doing a survey of this area. Have you a couple of minutes to answer me some questions, please?' If the answer is 'No', just say 'That's quite alright. Thank you' and go on to the next house.

5. If the householder asks where you are from or who you are doing the survey for, answer 'I am doing it for the . . . Church, but I didn't tell you that because I don't want you to slant your answers, I want you to be dead honest, whatever you feel'.

6. Begin at one end of a road and call house to house. Don't choose houses but take them as they come. About half the people will be out anyway. You may have agreed

to complete ten forms in each road so as to cover more roads but still take them as they come.

7. If people are silent when you have asked a question, be silent, comfortable and unembarrassed with them. Encourage by smiling, nodding or grunting agreement or appreciation but *never* suggest an answer.

8. When you get to the last question, and the answerer does not give a firm 'Yes', say, 'That's all the questions. Thank you very much for your answers. I am doing this survey for the . . . Church. They want to know what people think and feel in the area. Your answers will be treated as absolutely confidential but they will be most valuable. Thank you'.

9. If the answer to the last question is an emphatic 'Yes' by all means share something of your faith if you feel it right to do so. Say, 'That's all the questions. Thank you so much for your answers. Actually I am a Christian and I do know God in a personal way and that means all the world to me'. Add – shortly – a personal testimony or whatever else you feel to be right and genuine with that situation.

10. When you have left the house, place the house number and the road name on the top left-hand corner of the form. On the top right-hand corner place a quick description of the person visited, sex and rough estimate of age and anything else important – e.g. 'Lady, about forty, Asian' or 'Man, over 65, disabled'. This helps in interpreting the information and if there is to be any further follow up.

11. If invited in accept. Don't waste time but be grateful for a comfortable seat and (maybe) a cup of tea.

12. Don't visit after dark.

A suggested survey form

The following could be retyped (don't forget to leave gaps for answers!) and used as a basic neighbourhood survey form.

1. What are the best things about this neighbourhood? What do you like most about living here?

2. What are the worst things about this neighbourhood? Is there anything you don't like here?

3. How long have you lived here?

−1 year	11–20 years
1–5 years	21–30 years
6–10 years	Over 30 years

4. What is the most important thing in life for you? What do you live for?

5. What do you think is the main thing wrong with the world today?

6. How do you think it could be put right?

7. Do the churches here show much love and care to the people who do not go to church?
    (Do they show any love or care to you or contact you at all?)
    YES   DON'T KNOW   A LITTLE
    NO   SOME

8. Is God important in your life?
    YES   NO   SOMETIMES
    DON'T KNOW

9. If there was a way in which you could get to know God personally, would you want to know Him?
    YES   NO
    SOMETIMES   DON'T KNOW
    I DO KNOW HIM PERSONALLY

Appendix 3: Mission of Friendship Visiting

Mission of Friendship visiting is another method of house to house visitation on behalf of the church. The following should be noted.

1. It is wise to take some piece of literature with you to give to those you are visiting. Read carefully through your literature so that you know what is in it.

2. Pray before you set out. Remember the real work is that done by the Spirit of God. Ours is the simple part of just being friendly and making the bridge of love over which the Holy Spirit comes. Place yourself quietly in God's love and ask His blessing for those you are about to meet.

3. If you are given an information card about the family or families you are to visit, memorize it beforehand. Don't take it with you. Simply take the name and address.

4. If you are visiting in an evening, it is as well to cast your eye over the television programmes before you go and avoid the things (especially serials) likely to be very popular.

5. Take a pencil and notebook in your pocket or handbag – and, if you are likely to be out after dark, a torch.

6. Don't go with a prejudice ('These are not church people. Their lives just revolve around themselves and the television and the pools'.) They will in fact be ordinary folk to whom nobody has troubled to take the Good News before. Christ loves them and longs for them to

respond to His love. Let some of His love be in your heart.

7. What do we say when the door opens? If you have been given the name of the householder, greet them with a smile and the use of their name – 'Mr Smith?' It makes a link and also checks that your information is correct. Then tell your names and say you have come on behalf of the church who want to offer their friendship.

8. Get the one you are visiting to do as much of the talking as you can by asking simple questions – 'How long have you lived here?'; 'Are you glad you came here?'; 'Where did you come from?'; 'What family have you got?'; and so on. People like to be able to talk about themselves if someone is genuinely interested in them.

9. Be bright and cheerful whatever happens. Hostile people are very few indeed. Most will be more frightened of you than you are of them and what they will remember is the general impression you left. More than one person has been brought to church because the visitor 'was so nice and he seemed so happy'.

10. If you should have called at a wrong moment apologise, if possible make an appointment to call again, and go. Of course, if you can do anything to help in a moment of trouble do so.

11. Hand over the literature fairly early – it may well be your talking point in the early stages. Hand it over firmly – don't ask folk if they want it or offer it shyly.

12. Go into the house if you possibly can. When asked in, be delighted and say so, and thank them when you go.

13. It is probably wise not to visit after 9 pm. Whatever time you go, don't stay too late unless you are really wanted.

14. When you get into the house *relax*. One or two strange people sitting stiffly on the edge of their chairs looking like Mounties who have 'come to get their man' (really, of course scared out of their wits!) is enough to put anyone off for good.

15. If you are offered a cup of tea or coffee, take it and whatever it tastes like, treat it like nectar from the gods!

16. Above all *be yourself*. Folk who pretend cannot make real relationships because their interest and attention is on themselves.

17. Get it clear that your main job will be *listening*. Listen well, with sympathy and interest. Really look at the other person, meet with them, give them your attention and care sincerely about them with the care of Christ.

18. Avoid the appearance of being 'the religious type' and using religious attitudes and phrases. You are a Christian and you will not be afraid to speak of spiritual things when this is appropriate and required, but you will do so simply and in your own ordinary words.

19. Don't criticise other denominations or discuss the personal failings of particular church people or anyone else. It is not polite, not helpful – and it gets around!

20. If folk want to attack the church, don't give a heated defence of it. Some of what they say may well be true. Speak of Christ, admit that He is the only perfect One and we are only learners in His school.

21. *Don't argue*. From argument comes only bitterness, self-justification and increased hardness. Our part is to win the man, not the argument.

22. If anyone is rude to you, just don't mind – it is only your pride that can get hurt. When others are rude, arrogant or ill-tempered, Christians 'stay sweet'. Your attitudes and spirit are also speaking and speaking louder than your words.

23. Avoid being side-tracked into complicated discussions on secondary things ('Do you think it is wrong to have a big booze-up every Friday?'). Christ changed people's lives and gave them eternal worth and infinite meaning and He still does so today for those who give their lives to Him in trust and obedience and learn of Him. Our faith centres in a Person, not a set of rules.

24. If you are asked questions to which you do not know the answers, acknowledge it frankly. If necessary say

you will find out – and do so. A minister will, of course, gladly call on folk with real problems.

25. Regard your conversations with folk and any information they give as strictly confidential. Don't talk about it.

26. If any part of another's life and problems has been shared with you, and if circumstances are right, close with a short and simple prayer asking God's blessing on the people.

27. Close the gate behind you.

28. Pray for the people you have visited in your private prayers.

29. If you have made a genuine contact you may be able to follow it up with further friendliness, by asking them round to your home for an hour or by dropping in on them again. But make sure your friendship is natural and genuine. If your friends are going to come to church with you for the first time, meet them or call for them, sit with them and afterwards introduce them to the minister and to any Christians whose interests might be similar to their own.

30. Don't get discouraged if you do not get quick or spectacular results. Carry on faithfully praying, visiting and caring. Much may be done for Christ that you are not aware of. Even in the most unlikely visits the Holy Spirit may use the happy impression you left or some word you said to continue His own work in a human heart.

You do not use a questionnaire in Mission of Friendship visiting but it is helpful to write a brief report and include the following:

1. Name and address of person visited.

2. Details of any others in the home. Ages of children.

3. Whether any church background or connection.

4. Whether interested. Would you like to call again? Would you recommend one of you to call with someone else of similar situation or interests?

5. Is there any way we should help this family practically? Some loving touch like sending flowers?
6. Any other information relevant.
The report can then be submitted to those in your church responsible for pastoral care and follow up for the area in question.

Note: You are welcome to reproduce these hints for your church's use without bothering about copyright but please acknowledge their source.

Appendix 4: Discovering Our Gifts

Hints on discovering gifts

1. Small groups that have met weekly or fortnightly and worked together at depth are the best vehicle for discovering gifts. After about a year let them study together 1 Corinthians 12, Romans 12 and Ephesians 4. Then let each have a sheet of paper and put down on the left-hand side the names of everyone in the group (including their own) and then add beside each name the gifts that they think each person has been given. The papers are collected and someone reads out from them (for each person in turn) all that the others have observed about their gifts. Sometimes quite surprising discoveries are made in this way.

2. Any firm with as many employees as your church has members, would have a Personnel Officer or even a Personnel Department. Have you been given a wise and understanding member who could help others discover their gifts and begin to use them?

3. Ministers, deacons and elders who visit have opportunity to speak person to person and share the life situation of the other. Here is an opportunity to talk about gifts and perhaps discover them together.

4. When a new member joins the church, he will of course receive instruction in the Christian faith and life, and this will include something about gifts and their use. But it is a great help if every new member also has a sponsor, at least for his first year, who cares for him and

is able over a length of time to help him to discover his gifts.

5. The method below will be useful to those lacking other ways and as a supplement to other ways.

Note: It is not enough just to *discover* gifts. They also have to be used and developed. Some people have great musical ability, but this is unlikely to be expressed effectively without the hard grind of learning how to play an instrument.

Personal Gift Assessment

Read the following points and mark yourself out of 5 for each. If you give yourself 5 it will be one of your very strong points. If you give yourself 0 or 1 it will be one of your very weak points. Fill how many you give yourself in the square with the number.

1. I am good at listening.
2. I enjoy explaining things to others from the Bible.
3. I love preaching or talking about Jesus to a congregation or group.
4. I am often used to bring others to Christ.
5. I enjoy administrative work.
6. I feel a deep, caring love for those who are ill and a call to help them get well.
7. I am handy at most things and adaptable.
8. I am deeply concerned about the world and social affairs.
9. I am usually looked to for a lead.
10. I make helpful relationships with others easily.
11. Others are helped when I teach them things.
12. I love the study and work in preparing a message.
13. God has given me a great love for others and a longing to win them for Him.
14. I can organise well, clearly and efficiently.
15. Others find my presence soothing and healing.
16. I like helping other people

17. I am active in service in the community.
18. In a group I am often elected chairman or leader.
19. I can encourage others and help bear burdens.
20. I love study and finding the facts.
21. My sermons have been clearly blessed to others.
22. I find my life is full of opportunities to witness to Christ.
23. I love doing office work and do it thoroughly.
24. I have sometimes laid hands on the sick and they have been helped.
25. I am a practical type.
26. I am very aware of the needs of society today and feel called to do something about it.
27. When leading something I put a lot of preparation into it.
28. I really care about other people.
29. I have patience in helping others understand Christian things.
30. I feel a clear call to preach.
31. I love to talk to others about Jesus.
32. I am painstaking about details in organisation.
33. I spend time praying with and for sick people.
34. I spend much time helping others in practical ways.
35. I feel God is at work in the world today and I must work along with Him there.
36. I am good at delegating work to others in a team setting.

1	10	19	28	A
2	11	20	29	B
3	12	21	30	C
4	13	22	31	D
5	14	23	32	E
6	15	24	33	F

7	16	25	34	G
8	17	26	35	H
9	18	27	36	I

Add up the totals along each line and place them in the boxes marked A to I at the end of each line. Below is given the analysis of your score – for example if your highest total is in line E your gift is administration.

A – your gift is pastoral.
B – your gift is teaching.
C – your gift is preaching.
D – your gift is evangelism.
E – your gift is administration.
F – your gift is healing.
G – your gift is practical helping.
H – your gift is service to society.
I – your gift is leadership.

It is easy to mislead yourself and it may therefore be helpful to give a copy of this form to four of your closest friends and ask them to fill it in for you as honestly as possible. Don't show them your totals until after you have theirs. This form can be rewritten to include other fields of gifts. In every church there are rich resources unrecognised and unused. It takes time, care, love and prayer for them to be discovered, to unfold and be developed, but given the expectation and help in a loving, creative fellowship, the most wonderful things emerge even from the most unlikely people.

The church is to be alive in every member as the body in which Jesus lives and through which He reaches out and does His work.

Appendix 5

Have you heard of the four spiritual laws?

Just as there are physical laws that govern the physical universe,
so are there spiritual laws which govern your relationship with God.

Law one
God loves you, and offers a wonderful plan for your life.
  God's love 'For God so loved the world, that He gave His only begotten Son, that whoever believes in Him should not perish, but have eternal life'(John 3: 16)
  God's plan (Christ speaking) 'I came that they might have life, and might have it abundantly' (that it might be full and meaningful) (John 10: 10). *Why is it that most people are not experiencing the abundant life?*

Law two
Man is sinful and separated from God. Therefore, he cannot know and experience God's love and plan for his life.
  Man is sinful 'For all have sinned and fall short of the glory of God' (Romans 3: 23) Man was created to have fellowship with God; but, because of his stubborn self-will, he chose to go his own independent way and fellowship with God was broken. This self-will, characterised by an attitude of active rebellion or passive indifference, is evidence of what the Bible calls sin.

Man is separated 'For the wages of sin is death' (spiritual separation from God) (Romans 6: 23).

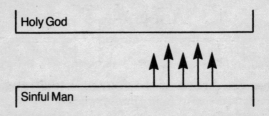

This diagram illustrates that God is holy and man is sinful. A great gulf separates the two. The arrows illustrate that man is continually trying to reach God and the abundant life through his own efforts, such as a good life, philosophy or religion. *The third law explains the only way to bridge this gulf.* . .

Law three

Jesus Christ is God's only provision for man's sin. Through Him you can know and experience God's love and plan for your life.

He died in our place 'But God demonstrates His own love toward us, in that while we were yet sinners, Christ died for us' (Romans 5: 8).

He rose from the dead 'Christ died for our sins . . . He was buried . . . He was raised on the third day, according to the Scriptures . . . He appeared to Peter, then to the twelve. After that He appeared to more than five hundred . . .' (1 Corinthians 15: 3–6).

He is the only way to God 'Jesus said to him, "I am the way, and the truth, and the life; no one comes to the Father, but through Me" ' (John 14: 6)

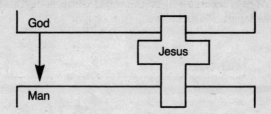

This diagram illustrates that God has bridged the gulf which separates us from Him by sending His Son, Jesus Christ, to die on the cross in our place to pay the penalty for our sins. *It is not enough to just know these three laws. . .*

Law four
We must individually receive Jesus Christ as Savior and Lord; then we can know and experience God's love and plan for our lives.

We must receive Christ 'But as many as received Him, to them He gave the right to become children of God, even to those who believe in His name' (John 1: 12).

We receive Christ through faith 'For by grace you have been saved through faith; and that not of yourselves, it is the gift of God; not as a result of works, that no one should boast' (Ephesians 2: 8,9).

When we receive Christ, we experience a new birth (Read John 3: 1–8.)

We receive Christ by personal invitation (Christ is speaking) 'Behold, I stand at the door and knock; if any one hears My voice and opens the door, I will come in to him' (Revelation 3: 20).

Receiving Christ involves turning to God from self (repentance) and trusting Christ to come into our lives, to forgive our sins and to make us the kind of people He wants us to be. Just to agree intellectually that Jesus Christ is the Son of God and that He died on the cross for our sins is not enough. Nor is it enough to have an

281

emotional experience. We receive Jesus Christ by faith, as an act of the will.

These two circles represent two kinds of lives.

SELF-DIRECTED LIFE
S – Self is on the throne
† – Christ is outside the life
● – Interests are directed
   by self, often resulting in
   discord and frustration

CHRIST-DIRECTED LIFE
† – Christ is in the life
   and on the throne
S – Self is yielding to Christ
● – Interests are directed
   by Christ, resulting
   in harmony with God's plan

Which circle best represents your life? Which circle would you like to have represent your life? The following explains how you can receive Christ:

You can receive Christ right now by faith through prayer. Prayer is talking with God. God knows your heart and is not so concerned with your words as He is with the attitude of your heart. The following is a suggested prayer:

'Lord Jesus, I need You. Thank You for dying on the cross for my sins. I open the door of my life and receive You as my Saviour and Lord. Thank You for forgiving my sins and giving me eternal life. Take control of the throne of my life. Make me the kind of person You want me to be.'

Does this prayer express the desire of your heart? If it does, pray this prayer right now, and Christ will come into your life, as he promised.

Notes

1. Published by Navpress 1980.
2. Produced by Argus Communications, DLM House, Edinburgh Way, Harlow, Essex CM20 2HL.
3. By C H Dodd, 1936.
4. Published by Hodder and Stoughton 1970. Cf Michael Green's popular writing on the same theme, *Evangelism – Now and Then*, published by IVP, 1979.
5. Cf Mark 1.1. Bear in mind the fact that Mark gives nearly one third of his Gospel to the last week of the life of Jesus.
6. Cf John 20: 21–22 and Acts 1: 8.
7. Cf Matthew 7: 21;27; 12: 50; 25: 31–46.
8. First published in *The English Review*, October 1911.
9. *Florence Allshorn* by J H Oldham, published by SCM, 1951, p. 28.
10. *Op. cit.* (see Note 1.)
11. In a sermon entitled 'Dominoes' in *The Silver Shadow* by F W Boreham (Epworth 1918).
12. See especially *The Bible in World Evangelism*, by A M Chirgwin published by SCM, 1954 and Wyvern Books 1961; also *Market Unlimited* by Neville Cryer, published by Hodder and Stoughton, 1972.
13. *The New Testament in Modern English* by J B Phillips, published, published by Geoffrey Bles, 1960.
14. *Good News* Bibles, testaments and Gospels (including Gospels with localised covers – eg. 'Good

News for Blanktown') are published cheaply by The Bible Society, Stonehill Green, Westlea, Swindon, Wilts SN5 7DG.

15. Creative Publishing, 6 Pembroke Road, Moor Park, Northwood, Middx HA6 2HR.

16. Available from most Christian bookshops or from Kingsway Publications, Lottbridge Drove, Eastbourne, East Sussex BN23 6NT.

17. Available from Christian Publicity Organisation, Garcia Estate, Canterbury Road, Worthing, West Sussex BN15 1BW. They also publish many tracts and leaflets which can be overprinted.

18. *The Four Spiritual Laws* is available from Campus Crusade for Christ, Arrowhead Springs, San Bernardino, California, CA92414, USA. See also Appendix 5 of this book.

19. *Knowing God Personally* is available from Campus Crusade, 103 Friar Street, Reading, Berks RG1 1EP.

20. Published by Cassell and Co, 1970.

21. 1 Peter 2: 5. Cf 1 Corinthians 3: 9, Ephesians 2: 22 and Hebrews 3: 6.

22. Ephesians 1: 23, 4: 12–16; 1 Corinthians 12: 12–27; Colossians 1: 18; Romans 12: 5.

23. Ray Stedman is the Pastor of Peninsula Bible Church, Palo Alto, California, author of *Body Life* and many other books.

24. John Goddard is minister of the Baptist church at Bloxham near Banbury. He was previously Adviser in Education to the Baptist Union in London.

25. This quotation appeared in an article in *Frontier* magazine, twenty years ago.

26. Published by Victor Books, Wheaton Illinois, USA and available from the Luis Palau Evangelistic Team, 175 Tower Bridge Road, London SE1 2AM.

27. *Three Times Three Equals Twelve* by Brian Mills (Kingsway Publications 1986).

28. The Evangelical Alliance, 186 Kennington Park Road, London SE11 4BT.
29. Fact and Faith Films, 120 The Roch, Bury, Lancashire BL9 0PJ.
30. Trinity Video Ltd, Grafton Place, Worthing, West Sussex BN11 1QX.
31. Evangelism Explosion information from 228 Shirley Road, Southampton SO1 3HR.
32. Grove Booklets, Bramcote, Notts NG9 3DS.
33. From *The Face of My Parish* by Tom Allen.
34. From the hymn *And didst Thou, Lord our sorrows take?* by T H Gill (1819–1906).
35. From the hymn *Rescue the Perishing*.
36. Published as a paperback by Fount Books and available through most bookshops.
37. What follows is an outline of the course for new Christians called *Food for Faith* by Lewis Misselbrook, available from the Baptist Union of Scotland, 14 Aytoun Road, Glasgow G41 5RT at £1.50.
38. See Appendix 4.
39. There are many books on groups. We recommend *How to Conduct Home Bible Classes* by Al Wollen, The Luis Palau Evangelistic Team, 175 Tower Bridge Road, London SE1 2AS.
40. *Your Church Can Grow* by Peter Wagner, published by Regal Books, 1976.
41. Material and courses from the Navigators can be obtained direct from Navpress, Tregaron House, 27 High Street, New Malden, Surrey KT3 4BY, or from Christian bookshops.
42. See address above.
43. *Op. cit.* (see Note 39.)
44. In *How to Plant Churches* ed. Monica Hill, published by MARC Europe for the British Church Growth Association.
45. Published by IVP, 1981.
46. Published by SCM, 1954. An alternative is *We Belong Together* by Bruce Milne, (IVP 1978).

47. *Op. cit.* (see Note 4.)
48. Published by University of Notre Dame Press, Indiana, USA, © 1966.
49. From a lecture by Dr Arthur Dakin, the President of the Bristol Baptist College, 1950.
50. *Op. cit.* (see Note 48.)
51. *Basic Principles of Biblical Counselling* and *Effective Biblical Counselling*, published by Marshall Pickering, 1975 and 1977.
52. Cf *The Training of the Twelve* by A B Bruce – old but still good reading – and *The Master Plan of Evangelism* by Robert Coleman (Fleming Revell Co. 1963).
53. The Ichthus Fellowship led by Roger Forster, Ichthus House, 116 Berry Vale, London SE23 2LQ.
54. Paul could urge Christians to become imitators of him as well as of the Lord. Could we? Cf 1 Thessalonians 1: 6, 1 Corinthians 4: 16 and 11: 1. We recommend that all church leaders do the Bible Society wider course, 'Person to Person' to help them be natural and competent in witnessing.
55. Groups originally founded in America for personal sharing, not solely therapeutic but this is a vital aspect. See also Cecil Osborne's books, including *The Art of Understanding Your Mate*, published by Zondervan, 1970.
56. *The Price and Power of Revival* by Duncan Campbell, published by The Faith Mission, Edinburgh.
57. For information on Prayer Triplets write to Brian Mills at The Evangelical Alliance (see address above).
58. See *Three Times Three Equals Twelve* (*op. cit.*).

If you wish to receive *regular information* about *new books*, please send your name and address to:

London Bible Warehouse
PO Box 123
Basingstoke
Hants RG23 7NL

Name..

Address ....

....

....

....

I am especially interested in:
- ☐ Biographies
- ☐ Fiction
- ☐ Christian living
- ☐ Issue related books
- ☐ Academic books
- ☐ Bible study aids
- ☐ Children's books
- ☐ Music
- ☐ Other subjects